Ida M. Tarbell

Ida M. Tarbell in a posed photograph meant to show her at work on "The History of the Standard Oil Company."

Ida M. Tarbell

The Woman Who Challenged
Big Business — and Won!

Emily Arnold McCully

Clarion Books • HOUGHTON MIFFLIN HARCOURT

BOSTON • NEW YORK

Clarion Books

215 Park Avenue South, New York, New York 10003

Clarion Books is an imprint of Houghton Mifflin Harcourt Publishing Company.

www.hmhco.com

The text was set in Minion.

Library of Congress Cataloging-in-Publication Data

McCully, Emily Arnold.

Ida M. Tarbell : the woman who challenged big business — and won! / by Emily Arnold McCully.

pages cm

Includes bibliographical references and index.

ISBN 978-0-547-29092-8 (hardcover)

1. Tarbell, Ida M. (Ida Minerva), 1857–1944 — Juvenile literature. 2. Journalists — United States — Biography —

Juvenile literature. [1. Tarbell, Ida M. (Ida Minerva), 1857–1944. 2. Journalists. 3. Women — Biography.] I. Title.

CURR PN4874.T23M33 2014

070.92 — dc23

[B]

2012039650

Manufactured in the U.S.A.

DOW 10 9 8 7 6 5 4 3

4500525399

For the investigative journalists of tomorrow

Contents

PART ONE

Preparation

CHAPTER ONE

The Oil Region

*I*DA MINERVA TARBELL, an eagerly awaited first child, was born on November 5, 1857, in a log house on her maternal grandparents' little dairy farm in Hatch Hollow, Pennsylvania. Ida's father was far away in Iowa. Her mother's dreams for the baby daughter were expressed in the names she chose: Ida, from a poem about a women's college, and Minerva, the goddess of wisdom.

Franklin and Esther Tarbell had married after a six-year courtship. Esther was liberally educated for a woman of the time, and both had taught school; as a man, Franklin earned four times what Esther did. He had also worked as a welder, a river pilot, and a carpenter. Now he had relocated again, leaving Esther, pregnant with their child, at her parents' farm. He was making a homestead on Iowa's fertile soil, so superior to western Pennsylvania's.

Ida's grandmother was a frontier snob, given to reminding Esther that she came from one of the best families and was a descendant of Sir Walter Raleigh, of the first American Episcopal bishop, and of a member of General Washington's staff. Esther would take up this

*Esther and Ida on Ida's first
birthday, November 5, 1858.*

theme with her own children, telling them never to forget who they were. Franklin was descended from hardy, self-reliant New Englanders who had fought wars and cleared land and were not famous or grand. Earlier generations had moved from Massachusetts and New Hampshire to New York, where Franklin was born, then to Pennsylvania.

Conditions in 1857 didn't favor another new beginning. While Iowa's white population had grown sixfold in a decade, Sioux warriors still attacked settlers in revenge for the loss of their lands. Iowa winters were much harsher than those most immigrants had ever known. Still, Franklin found a great deal to praise about his new surroundings and described the immensity of flat prairie, its birds and flowers, the sight of wagon trains bearing families farther west.

Franklin was an introspective, judgmental man of powerful religious convictions. The calm demeanor instilled by his Christian faith gave way to manic bursts of activity. He had a great taste for travel and adventure, a sense of fun, and a gift for storytelling that captivated his children. Tall and spare, he was vain enough to cover his early baldness with a wig. While he built their new house, he whistled "from morning 'til night, mischief and tenderness chasing each other across his blue eyes as he thought of [Esther's] coming, their future together."

The Tarbells had expected that their first child would be born an Iowan. But it was not to be. The country entered an economic depression in 1857. In Iowa, railroad lines and construction projects were left unfinished. The Tarbells' bank collapsed, wiping out their savings. A disheartened Franklin realized he would have to abandon his unfinished house and go back to Hatch Hollow. Unable to pay for transportation, he began to walk the thousand miles through Illinois, Indiana, and Ohio in the fall of 1858. It took him eighteen months. To pay for food and shelter, he taught in rural schools as he went.

Meanwhile, her adoring grandmother was indulging little Ida Minerva, and no one was competing for her mother's attention. Her first two and a half years of life were so happy, she remembered them later as a lost idyll. Ida spent her days scampering through pastures bright with wildflowers. Lambs, calves, kittens, and puppies were her playmates. She was developing a precocious passion for freedom and beauty.

She had never before laid eyes on the ragged man who appeared on the doorstep and embraced her mother. Ida cried, "Go away, bad man!"

Franklin still hoped to make good in Iowa. He took a job as a flatboat pilot to earn money so that his wife and daughter could move there with him. But the fall of 1859 was one of the great turning points in modern history. The Tarbells' lives were set on an unexpected new course.

—— ✳ ——

Petroleum, or oil, as we know it, is organic waste that has been pressure-cooked deep in the earth over millennia and turned into hydrocarbons: oil and natural gas. Seneca Indians traditionally skimmed the inky green substance from ponds and streams and rubbed it on their bodies to treat aches and pains. White settlers, including Franklin Tarbell, learned to use it too, soaking up surface oil with blankets, wringing them out, and applying the stinking ooze to their joints and machinery alike. Some even drank it to prevent colds. A 1755 map of western Pennsylvania labels the area *Petroleum* and identifies one of the waterways there as Oyl Creek. Oil floated regularly on the creek and was sold as a patent medicine called Seneca Oil.

Edwin Drake (in top hat) and an unidentified man
with Drake's famous well in the background, 1859.

Seeping into the crevices in rock, and often sealed under a layer of salt water, oil was considered an undesirable byproduct released when salt was drilled.

In the 1850s, whale oil, then the principal fuel for lamps, was becoming scarce, as whales had been overhunted. Coal oil (kerosene distilled from petroleum) was a common substitute, but it was smoky and smelly, and the flame went out when a coal-oil lamp was carried from room to room. A chimney lamp invented in Europe made coal kerosene more practical, but coal oil clogged lamp parts and was unsafe to use in confined spaces.

After one of a group of investors visited western Pennsylvania in 1853 and reported the region's promise, a sample of oil was sent to a chemist at Yale University, who determined that oil could be refined into lamp fuel. This made oil a potentially profitable resource. The investors decided to try adapting a derrick used to drill for underground salt to see if it could recover large quantities of oil from deep underground recesses.

Edwin Drake, an unemployed former railroad worker who had a train pass and therefore could travel for free, was recruited to go to Titusville. On behalf of his investors, he bought a hardscrabble farm in that timbered wasteland to try out the drill. Months of failure followed. The locals thought he was crazy. The derrick he put up was known as Drake's Folly.

In August 1859, a blacksmith hired by Drake to operate the drill succeeded in striking oil. Washtubs, whiskey barrels, molasses crocks, anything that would catch flow from the oil fountain, or geyser, were hustled into service. The oil rush — in what was popularly called "Oildorado" — had begun. Just a decade after the gold rush, this new frenzy would outdo it by far, largely determining the course of America's economic history for the succeeding century and a half.

Would-be oil prospectors left their farms, law offices, stores, and mills and poured into the region. Farms around Titusville that had recently been bought for $25,000 now sold for as much as $1,600,000. Many were sliced into little pieces and leased to oil hunters for whatever the traffic would bear. It is said that one cunning yokel, offered a ¼ percent royalty payment for his plot, held out for ⅛ percent, thinking that was bigger. The whole region was up for grabs. Derricks, or drills, appeared wherever a piece of ground could be exploited. The first wells were dug with "spring poles," simple devices driven into the earth by human and horse power. The oil had to be collected in vessels, then transported to a cobbled-together refinery to be heated to separate it into useful components, such as kerosene. Roads were scraped out of the mud, shacks thrown up for men to sleep in. Oil was flowing so fast that prospectors couldn't collect it all.

Related ways to make money quickly presented themselves. Housing, food, banking, legal services, and entertainment had to be provided for the prospectors. Swindlers found their own opportunities. Overrun by greedy interlopers with only one thing in mind — money! — locals felt that human nature itself had gone bad. A few, however, saw divine intervention at work. God had apparently chosen to bestow upon the citizens of northwestern Pennsylvania unheard-of riches.

A farm given over to oil derricks. The owner, John Benninghoff, made a lot of money from the oil discovered on his land but lost most of it to thieves in 1868.

Prospectors soon learned that instant wealth could be wiped out just as quickly as it appeared, when oversupply caused prices to plummet or when thieves took a hand. Once forced to the surface, oil was sometimes stolen. Wells were spied on, and if they were productive, their output was siphoned away underground by a derrick planted nearby. With no authority to rein them in, men drank, brawled, and whored. Upright citizens organized vigilantes to keep order.

Franklin Tarbell learned of Drake's successful strike as word raced across the region. A natural entrepreneur, Franklin saw that there would be an urgent need for vessels to store and transport the gushing oil. He designed wooden tanks that would hold two hundred to six hundred barrels of oil and showed them to men on the Rouse farm, site of an early strike. When Rouse placed a large order, he set up shop, ordered lumber, and went to fetch his family. Despite the chaotic atmosphere in the region, Franklin believed he could manage a family life, even provide some comfort and respectability for his wife, and reap the rewards of the oil business at the same time. For the most part, he succeeded.

As the Tarbell wagon, loaded with the family's possessions, rolled through oil country, new baby William in Esther's arms, Ida watched with wide eyes. Oil was everywhere. Geysers spilled over. Barrels and wagons dribbled their contents. Stumps abounded where trees had been hacked down to build wells, shacks, and, eventually, hotels and sidewalks. Men carried planks so they could cross the muck dry shod.

The family pulled onto the flats next to a creek called Cherry Run, where twenty-five oil wells per acre were already operating. Franklin built a shack and a workshop, and Ida found herself plumb in the middle of the oil rush.

The modest Tarbell dwelling was surrounded by oily sand, oily pits, and puddles and dumps of oily gravel regurgitated by the drills. Every living

An oil town.

thing was slathered black with oil and tar and smelled abominable. Nothing was ever cleaned up, not spilled crude, broken equipment, dead horses and mules, or human and animal waste. Wells that failed were simply abandoned. If a barrel sank, retrieving it was too much trouble. The few trees not felled for tanks or to house oil wells poked spectrally through a smog that reeked nauseatingly of gas and throbbed with the shrieks and squeals of engines and pile drivers and the curses of men. Teamsters' wagons crowded the throughways, and their flatboats clogged the waters of Oil Creek. None of the muck ever dried up or froze. When wagons sank into the mud above their axles, they were left there, as were the pitiable horses, their coats rubbed to bare skin. Everything was expendable in pursuit of the fortunes to be made.

Ida desperately missed the farm, her grandmother's love, and her mother's undivided attention. The world she'd been dropped into offended her tender sensibilities deeply. Her parents had robbed her of joy, with no explanation. The shock marked her forever. Late in life she wrote, "No industry of man in its early days has ever been more destructive of beauty, order, decency, than the production of petroleum."

Even worse, she was stripped of her independence. For a child who had freely wandered over the endlessly interesting barnyard and meadows of a small family farm, the restrictions were onerous. Ida was warned never to climb the enticing derrick, rising like a giant magic ladder, in the front yard. Will did climb it once, his baby skirts flying in the breeze. A panicked Esther was told to keep still while a driller gently talked him down. Ida wasn't ever to venture below their house, ringed by open pits of oil. She got a spanking when she disobeyed, which was often, because she was unquenchably curious.

Just after her third birthday, Ida announced to her mother that she was

Ida in the early 1860s. Her mother dressed her with care, and she appreciated pretty clothes.

going back to her grandma and stomped out the door. Esther watched her go without comment. The little girl with dark brown hair and earnest gray eyes followed the route she had seen her father's men take after work. A ridge ran along the horizon at the far side of the valley. She trudged toward it. It became harder and harder to lift her feet. The closer she got to the ridge, the higher it looked. Even worse, she realized she didn't know the way to her grandmother's after all.

The sun was going down. She looked behind her: the Tarbell shanty was barely visible in the distance, a light shining in a window. It drew her back.

Pausing outside the door, she had to admit defeat. She wasn't free, couldn't make her own way. Still, she had demonstrated headstrong bravery that had yielded to reality. The little prodigal received neither a lecture nor punishment, just a matter-of-fact welcome and a warmed-over supper. She wrote later that her respect for her mother was established that night. When Ida faced difficulties later on, she pictured her small self before the black mountain, looking longingly back to a lighted window. She would never again take on a challenge without fully preparing for it.

One other self-revealing episode stuck in Ida's memories of that time. It was her first attempt to test a hypothesis by experiment. Her curiosity naturally led her toward science, and now she attempted to pursue its method.

Her father's workshop sat next to a creek. Ida had been told never to play in it, but she loved to watch its noisy currents and store up observations. She tossed a pebble into the water. It sank. On the other hand, leaves floated. A question entered her three-year-old mind and would not budge: Was her brother, a baby still in dresses, a floater or a sinker? She couldn't tell by looking. The more she pondered the question, the more urgently she needed to know the answer. She thought of a way to find out. She led the unsuspecting Will to the footbridge and dropped him into the creek.

The baby's skirts billowed out and buoyed him. He howled. One of Franklin's men dashed over and pulled him out of the water. At eighty, Ida still remembered the "peace of satisfied curiosity" she felt having discovered that her brother "belonged to the category of things that floated." She couldn't remember whether she'd been spanked after the episode. After all, Will hadn't drowned.

How her life would have changed had Will drowned is another matter.

CHAPTER TWO

Burning Curiosity

*I*DA ALWAYS REMEMBERED rolling in the sweet-smelling wood shavings in her father's barrel shop with Will, and planting shavings like curls in her brother's hair. But vivid images of tragedy also marked her early childhood. Ida's parents tried to shield her from the worst violence, but that only made her want to discover the truth about it for herself.

She was barely four on the day in 1861 when her father was at the local hotel, discussing the attack on Fort Sumter that had sparked the Civil War. A man dashed in, shouting, "Gusher! It's the big one!" Henry Rouse had bored deeper than usual and it had paid off. The men rushed from the hotel, Franklin Tarbell mentally estimating how many tanks would be needed to collect the oil. Within minutes, 150 men had gathered to see the lucky geyser.

Suddenly, a sheet of fire enveloped them, followed by a tremendous explosion. Oil continued to pour out of the well and ignite when it hit the ground. Fire blazed over an acre containing two wells, one hundred full barrels, several open vats, and a barn. Oil drilling was

An oil well burns out of control.

hazardous; this was the disaster they had all known to guard against, but now the worst had occurred.

That night, a shaken Franklin told his wife what had happened. Nineteen men had burned to death, including Rouse. Nobody knew how many others were injured. Their children safe in bed, the sleepless Tarbells talked softly of the horror. Hearing shuffling outside, Franklin opened the door to a swaying creature so charred and swollen it hardly looked human. This was one of their friends, they learned, when he managed to utter his name.

Esther turned the parlor into a hospital, and under her care the man eventually recovered. As Ida recalled, "The relics of that tragedy were long about our household — comforters and bed quilts she had pieced and quilted for Iowa stained with linseed oil, used to treat burns, but too precious to be thrown away." Late in her life, the incident seemed to her like something she had read in a book, and only in hindsight did she appreciate what the many weeks of caring for the man must have been like for Esther.

In the oil region, life could be ended in a heedless instant. Not long after the disaster, three neighborhood women were incinerated when one of them poured oil on what she thought were dead coals. Ida "heard horrified whisperings about [her]. Their refusal to tell [her] aroused a terrible curiosity." Guessing that the bodies were laid out in a nearby home, the little girl slipped in and lifted a sheet to look at them. The hideous sight kept her from sleeping soundly for weeks. The effect was long lasting; as an old woman, she began to scream when a filling-station attendant accidentally spilled gasoline on her.

Despite these fatalities right next door, Ida called the death of President Abraham Lincoln, when she was seven, her first realization of tragedy. She recalled the day her father returned, terribly downcast; her mother asked what was wrong, then burst into tears and ran sobbing to her bedroom. Her parents hung black crape over their door. The power of an event that had happened far away to someone they'd never met astonished and puzzled Ida. The world was wider than she'd realized, and the ripples of its events could be felt even at home, could touch even *her*.

Their town was now called Rouseville. "It changed from a huddle of shanties on a muddy, disorderly flat to an orderly town with shops, a bank, a hotel, a square, homes, schools scattered over the hills," Ida recollected. "The change was due to the fact that my Mother and her friends had taken an active and intelligently directed part in seeing that the community into which they had been so accidentally dropped was a fit place to bring up children, a fit place for self-respecting families." Esther joined with other women to civilize the town and keep disorderly elements at bay. One dark night, Rouseville's women got their men to set the gambling and prostitution "joy boat" *Floating Palace* adrift, carrying its inebriated passengers downstream.

As soon as Franklin was convinced the oil business was going to last, he built his family a house high on an uncleared hillside that was too steep for drilling. When in leaf, the trees there concealed the derricks and shanties below. Eight-year-old Ida's freedom was restored! She rode Flora, the family horse, through flowered meadows and below arching trees. She climbed the trees, pretending to be a pirate in her crow's nest. She attended a school organized by a Mrs. Rice, whom she recalled as one of her best teachers. At home, where the family subscribed to the best magazines, she and Will pored over stories and engravings that let them imagine orderly, protected bourgeois communities.

The huge gushers that in 1865 established the short-lived boomtown of Pithole, a few miles away, brought new business to Franklin. He commuted there on horseback, carrying large amounts of cash in his pockets, which caused Esther frantic worry when he was late. Ida kept vigil in the night with her mother, partly for support, but largely because the suspense was so exciting. Ida wanted no part of her mother's anxious handwringing. She imagined her father as a romantic, heroic figure on a charger and never doubted that he

Ida, around 1865.

would be returning home. Franklin always made it safely past the brigands of the night.

Pithole was drilled dry in five hundred days, and instantly the instant metropolis was no more. Iron tanks began replacing wooden ones, so Franklin switched gears and joined the oil drillers.

As barrels to hold the stuff had helped propel the production of oil when Franklin moved to Cherry Run, pipelines and tank cars on rails revolutionized its transport by 1866. The cutthroat competition for dominance would focus on these means of moving oil to markets.

The prospering Tarbell family grew. A sister named Sarah was born in 1863, followed two years later by another brother, "Little Frankie." When Ida was eleven, Sarah and Frankie caught scarlet fever, the most dreaded childhood illness. Ida was barred from entering their room, but she hovered in the hall, desperate to keep their brave little spirits from escaping to heaven. Frankie fought the doctor and shrieked in terror, then died. This memory was so painful that when Ida began writing her autobiography, she could hardly bear to think about it and told a colleague that she wanted to leave it out of the book.

Sarah survived the disease. Relieved and grief stricken, but told that it was all God's will, Ida began her struggle with Christian doctrine. Heaven was presented to her as the surest thing in life. Could Frankie really have gone there? She had only a saccharine Sunday school illustration to help her visualize it. When the Old Testament book of Genesis was read in church, she tried to picture the six days of creation and the seventh day of rest. The minister said it was all true. Ida wondered.

More subject to examination were the sins of the booming new town of Petroleum Center, which was not patrolled by respectable citizens. Visiting there as a young adolescent, Ida could cast sidelong glances at brothels and

Left to right: Ida, Sarah, and Will.

"feed [her] curiosity about things in the world about which [she] was not supposed to know." She also went questing behind the bunkhouse where her father's workers slept. These men ate meals with the family, with Esther on guard against any vulgarity they might introduce. What were they like when not subject to her mother's rules?

A brief search under a pile of leaves yielded a bonanza: discarded copies of the *Police Gazette,* a popular men's magazine with sensational illustrated stories of vice and crime. Here were depicted depravities that Ida knew existed right in Petroleum Center but were not discussed at home. Whenever a move was made to establish a saloon in Rouseville, her mother would mutter, "Let them go to Petroleum Center." One visitor remarked that "the orgies in Petroleum Center sometimes eclipsed Monte Carlo and the Latin Quarter combined," referring to famous places for gambling and off-color entertainments. But details were left to Ida's imagination. Years later, Esther would tell her, "I indured [sic] enough at Rouseville for all the rest of my life." Esther's attempts to shield her children from wickedness were, at least in Ida's case, futile.

Ida shared the *Police Gazette* with an unnamed friend who was most likely Laura Seaver, the daughter of Franklin's business partner. Ida referred to Laura as probably the most intimate friend she ever had. At that stage in her life Ida was unguarded; both youngsters were avidly searching the world around them for clues to the forbidden and sharing their naive perceptions. Ida never lost touch with Laura or with other friends from her adolescence.

Ida soaked up knowledge and responded with grateful affection to adults who took an interest in her. Over the years, these mentors were mostly fatherly men. The father of another friend, Ida Hess, escorted Ida to his derrick-forested farm on a pair of fine saddle horses. The oil man clearly took a shine to the eager young girl, telling her at poetic length about the constellations and their legends. Her own father was a source of affection and entertainment. He whistled, sang, played a harmonica, and told wonderful stories. Ida associated his after-dinner cigar with contentment and storytelling.

The Tarbell family was happiest on vacation. Ida spent much of every summer at the Hatch Hollow farm with her mother and siblings. On special occasions they went fifty miles by train to Chautauqua Lake with a picnic. Ida wrote later that the social life of most Americans in those days could not be understood without an appreciation of the hold picnics had on them, the elaborate equipment involved, and the extensive menus. From the Mayville station at one end of the lake, the family would board a steamer that took them to Jamestown, where her father had gone to school. The trip was adventure enough, but to share it with a nostalgic father on holiday must have been magical. They stopped sometimes at a Methodist camp meeting, where worshipers gathered under a tent, prayed, sang hymns, and made spontaneous utterances of their faith, but "[the Tarbells] never liked it so well as going to Jamestown; neither did [Ida's] father." Still, Franklin soon joined the growing colony called Chautauqua, which was on its way to becoming a great American institution devoted to education and self-improvement and was the first steppingstone in Ida's career.

CHAPTER THREE

Defining Herself

*T*HE TARBELLS' CHURCH forbade dancing, theater, and card games. When Ida was small, she and her siblings played ball, leap-frog, jump rope, hopscotch, and hide-and-seek. Indoors, they played dominoes, Parcheesi, checkers, and backgammon. As she got older, Ida began to prefer solitary pursuits that took her far from home. The natural world fascinated her. She collected rocks, insects, and frogs in jars, and pressed flowers into scrapbooks. Her mother complained about the litter.

Ida was supposed to help out with the housework but often managed to be absent when duty called. She wrote fondly in later life about household rituals such as the ones that surrounded buying fabrics, being fitted by a dressmaker, and burning the leftover scraps. She referred to the seamstress as an autocrat, and clearly Esther was one too. Esther considered mere housework, especially in the primitive backwater where they lived, a waste of her education and talents, not to mention her heritage. Yet she was condemned to housewifery alone. She was probably proud of Ida's driving curiosity and independence, but she may have resented those qualities too. Ida rejected the housewife model for herself. The Tarbell home saw happy times, but Esther was not a fulfilled woman, and Ida knew it.

Both parents did their best to give their children an appreciation for culture. Despite his church's prohibitions, Ida's father took her to see actor Joseph Jefferson's famous portrayal of Rip Van Winkle. The Tarbells bought a piano, which Ida claimed had the mellowest tone of any she ever heard. She took lessons with various itinerant teachers and became adept enough to play for assemblies in high school.

The family was dedicated to their church. There were more Methodists in Rouseville than members of any other sect, so the town built a Methodist church. The Presbyterian Tarbells then converted to Methodism. In backwoods areas Methodists were known for their rowdy revivalist camp meetings. The congregation of Ida's church was scandalized by the so-called shouting method, but people did "come forward" to give themselves over to God. When Ida was about ten, she followed the crowd of repenters to the altar rail. Piously kneeling there, she was "keenly conscious . . . that the long crimson ribbons which hung from [her] hat must look

Ida and her father, 1867.

beautiful on [her] cream-colored coat. The realization of this hypocrisy cut to the heart."

Ida found humor in this recollection, but at the time she was powerfully influenced by her parents' strict faith. She very much feared being a sinner, and when she wrestled with doctrine, it was a terrifying contest. For a long time she believed herself the only person to harbor an impish inner voice that contradicted the pleasantries she uttered, and this filled her with guilt.

In 1870, Ida turned thirteen, and her family moved from Rouseville to the area's metropolis, Titusville, population 10,000. Franklin was doing well. He and Hess had struck oil on the Shoup farm, and the well produced a steady eighty barrels a day. Franklin bought the Bonta House, a hotel in the deserted town of Pithole, for $600. It had been built with French windows, a veranda, balconies, and a tower room for $60,000. Franklin hauled it away in pieces and put it up again in Titusville for his family to live in.

Ida's childhood home in Titusville. Her tower room is at left.

Esther could finally hold tea parties for women friends. Now the Tarbell children were surrounded by a cordon of respectability, for Titusville predated the oil rush and had a culture that offered newspapers, churches, and other institutions that separated it from the grime and vulgarity of the new industry. There were all kinds of stores and even a men's literary society that sponsored lectures. The streets had been graded and the light from gas lamps shone on sidewalks. Prominent musicians appeared at the opera house in the Parshall Hotel. A railroad made Titusville the main shipping center and entry point for the oil business.

It was the good schools that first drew the Tarbells to the town. Ida had learned all she could from the only teacher in Rouseville. She entered the crowded eighth grade a stranger among youngsters who all knew one another. The teacher, Mrs. Mary French, hardly glanced at her. Ida had engaged in a great deal of self-examination and at age thirteen felt she knew who she was: an independent seeker of the truth. So it was insulting to be ignored.

Ida soon discovered that she could skip school and head into the countryside without anyone stopping her. She repeated her pattern of exploring, collecting specimens from nature, and reading whatever lay at hand. Every now and then she showed up at school for a day. Her truancy seemed to be her secret. Her brother, Will, also spent long hours alone, fishing for trout or hunting, but he did his lessons effortlessly and excelled at them. Little Sarah, who had survived scarlet fever, often missed school because of illness. She was allowed to do as she pleased.

One day, when Ida had slipped into school for a token visit, Mrs. French suddenly turned on her and delivered a stinging lecture. It was a disgrace, she said, for a bright girl to be too wild to go to school and learn her lessons. Ida was astonished. The woman had noticed her all along, and not in a good way! Ida was shocked into reforming. "I suppose," she wrote, quoting from the Declaration of Independence, "that here a decent respect for the opinions of mankind was born; at least I became on the instant a model pupil." Ida always credited Mrs. French with waking her up to the importance of school.

By the end of her first year of high school, Ida was number one on the honor roll. Once at the top of the class, she had to stay there. She regarded it as a game, nothing to do with her life. But then she came to a turning point. "Suddenly . . . I found in certain textbooks the [open] sesame which was to free my curiosity, stir desires to know, set me working on my own to find out more than these books had to offer." The textbooks were for zoology, geology, botany, natural philosophy, and chemistry. She was especially fascinated by the idea of "growth." Thinking about the beginning of life, tadpoles becoming frogs, and evolution kept her awake at night.

From early childhood she'd wondered about the literal meaning of the Bible but had been afraid to question passages such as the story of creation in the book of Genesis. Now, spurred by her avid interest in science, she found Hugh Miller's *Testimony of the Rocks* in her father's library and read that the creation of the world had taken eons, not days. She was struck by unnerving doubt. Why did the Bible state so explicitly what had happened in a week, when the evidence in nature contradicted it? "A Bible that needed reconciling, that did not mean what it said, was not the rock I had supposed my feet were on," she acknowledged.

Eager to know the truth about the origin of life, Ida next entertained the idea of evolution with horror and amazement. Man's descent from the apes rather than from Adam and Eve was heresy to her family. But as usual, she didn't flinch at the idea.

Ida was not alone in questioning the Bible's account of creation. *The*

Testimony of the Rocks, published in 1857, had prepared readers for Darwin's *On the Origin of Species* in 1859. Darwin proposed that the great diversity of life on earth had a common origin and that the various species evolved through natural selection of characteristics favoring survival. His book had been avidly discussed in America and frequently denounced from pulpits as blasphemous. The descent of man from other animals was considered an affront to the ideas of God's plan and of man created in God's image. Christianity taught that life was unchanging, subject only to divine will.

A few Christian thinkers did accept Darwin's premise, theorizing that God actually had a role in evolution. God had created creatures capable of self-improvement; thus, evolution could account for the spiritual nature of mankind and for free will. Fortunately for Ida, the pastor of the Methodist church in Titusville was such a Christian. The Reverend Amos Norton Craft, an intellectually curious divine who spent a hefty portion of his salary on books, instituted a lecture series in the early 1870s meant to reconcile Genesis and geology. Ida was in eager attendance. The first topic was the universe. "I had never known there was [a universe]," Ida wrote later. "The stars, yes. I could name planets and constellations and liked nothing better than to lie on my back and watch them; but a universe with figures of its size was staggering. I went away from those Sunday night lectures fascinated, horror-stricken, confused — a most miserable child, for not only was my idea of the world shattered, not only was I left dizzily gyrating in a space to which there was no end, but the whole Christian system I had been taught was falling in a general ruin."

For a girl devoted to reason, science would almost certainly win out over faith. Science, exciting and dangerous, engaged Ida's developing intellect, while in her opinion faith required only passive submission. Ida was constitutionally incapable of hypocrisy, so she concluded she'd have to leave the church. But what could replace it? Every value she tried to live by came from the Bible. All the Tarbells were acutely, if inarticulately, aware of one another's sensitivities. The family kept conflict at bay by adhering to the precepts of "Do unto others" and "Turn the other cheek," which were Christian, not scientific. Science offered no such moral guidance.

Ida cared deeply about being good. How was science going to help her? She didn't know. She'd been emptied of belief and filled with terrible doubt. But having to find answers on her own would eventually build intellectual self-confidence. Science did offer something momentous and lasting: the pursuit of knowledge.

How had life begun? How did things grow and change? Ida decided that she needed a microscope to examine life at its most elemental; she might even learn the secret of creation. She saved her money and bought one. Then she begged to be given the tower room at the top of the house for her laboratory. From now on, she would verify anything she was told. On the floors below, her family still believed that the world had been created in six days.

Reverend Craft's sermons prompted Ida to read a new magazine, *Popular Science Monthly,* the editor of which was eagerly promoting the ideas of English philosopher Herbert Spencer. Darwin had shown that natural selection could not guarantee improvement in a species or organism. The process was random, blind, and morally neutral. Applying the general idea of evolutionary change to human society, Spencer coined the phrase "survival of the fittest." His theory, called Social Darwinism, assumed that evolving societies did progress. Survival of the fittest meant survival of the best. This led to the conclusion that governments shouldn't intervene to solve economic or social problems, lest they impede the ascension of the fittest individuals. Not only was it wrong for governments to raise up the poor (or least fit), but public schools were, in Spencer's opinion, "useless and destructive" because they represented an attempt to alter the natural hierarchy of societies.

Spencer's ideas appealed to many Americans. The United States had conquered the North American continent from coast to coast, removing and killing Indian tribes and waging war against Mexico, under the banner of Manifest Destiny, a slogan that meant white Anglo-Saxons had the right to pursue progress everywhere. "Inferior" peoples simply wasted such opportunities. Spencer's philosophy suited this triumphalist frame of mind perfectly.

Supporters of Social Darwinism decreed that the nation could have either liberty or equality, but not both at the same time, and they chose liberty. The pursuit of individual self-interest would benefit society as a whole. Although the accumulation of great wealth by the few meant suffering for the many, it was a natural process and was meant to be.

Ida searched *Popular Science Monthly* for scientifically based rules of behavior that could replace the biblical injunctions that her parents followed. She found nothing of the sort.

At the Chautauqua summer meeting, a kind of educational fair held on the grounds of the Methodist Camp Meeting, two female scientists gave a demonstration of the microscope, which had recently undergone improvements and was now an instrument fit for conducting modern scientific investigation. Ida worked up her nerve and shyly confided that she, too, wanted to become a microscopist. Could she have a look and would they advise her? The ladies curtly rebuffed her. She was not to touch their device! Humiliated, Ida vowed to "show them." She let years pass before asking "for any special treatment at Chautauqua." But she remained as determined as ever to pursue science. "The quest of the truth had been born in me — the most tragic and incomplete, as well as the most essential of man's quests," she later wrote. Her passion for truth carried with it an insistence on forging her own way. This meant overcoming the limitations society placed on women.

Esther Tarbell had attended female academies and been certified to teach school. She'd been young when the campaign for equal rights for women first blossomed. Life in Rouseville was so isolated and fraught with the need to simply keep her family clean and safe that Esther had lost touch with the crusading women who crisscrossed the country, lecturing and organizing for women's right to vote, to work, to own property, and to divorce.

During the Civil War, women had put aside their campaign for equal rights. In 1868, the Fourteenth Amendment to the Constitution was passed, awarding the vote to Negro males but not to females of any race. Suffragists were outraged, and the suffrage movement was reignited. In her autobiography, Ida called those who carried on the campaign during her teenage years "splendid." But she never forgave a group who came to Esther's Titusville parlor and ignored her. In addition, the movement's leaders, Elizabeth Cady Stanton and Susan B. Anthony, declared their support for Victoria Woodhull, notorious clairvoyant, stockbroker, free love advocate, and self-proclaimed presidential candidate in 1872. An infamous hussy, in the view of Titusville ladies, Woodhull inspired more priggish gossiping than debate. Ida had no patience for that. If the visiting campaigners had bothered to share the best of their ideas with her, they might have made her a convert.

When the brilliant and scandalous Woodhull exposed the Reverend Henry Ward Beecher's alleged seduction of married women in his congregation, newspapers featured the scandal for months. Beecher was the most famous man in America, his sister the equally famous Harriet Beecher Stowe, author of *Uncle Tom's Cabin.* The *Police Gazette* ran more pieces

A cartoon from Harper's Weekly *depicts Victoria Woodhull as a devil tempting a debauched couple with the false salvation of "Free Love."*

about "The Woodhull" than about any other celebrity or event, spiced with pictures of the stereotypical "fast woman" in short skirts and suggestive poses. Mothers complained that their children grabbed the newspapers to devour the juicy details before their parents could stop them. Ida, too, read every word, becoming even more disenchanted with a women's rights movement that had gotten mixed up in such an affair.

It seemed to Ida that women were no more subjugated than men were. Each sex had its grievances. Most women she knew cared nothing for politics. Why should they be given the vote?

The principal "unfairness" at the Tarbell home involved household finances. Franklin's income varied along with the price of oil. He kept his wife in the dark about how much money he had, so although Esther was frugal, she sometimes inadvertently ran up debts. It was only when Esther had overspent that the couple talked about money, so for Ida the whole subject was fraught and their arrangement plainly destructive. Her father seemed to relish the power his control of money gave him. Ida noticed that her mother experienced considerable nervous strain, which she relieved by sewing and knitting. When still a young teenager, Ida vowed that she would make herself financially independent. She was aware that if she managed to do that, it would have to be in a man's world. That was fine with her; the men she knew showed much more friendly interest in her than most women did.

It may seem surprising that the suffragist crusaders' compelling arguments for women's rights didn't appeal to Ida's sense of fair play. But the Woodhull-Beecher scandal overshadowed the struggle for equality. Approaching womanhood, already beginning to imagine living a life very different from her mother's, Ida found the public shenanigans and the gossiping an embarrassing symptom of weakness. The emphasis on sex must have made her uncomfortable. The conclusion she drew from her short lifetime of observation was that wedlock was bondage and she must avoid it, along with its physical expression of love, at all costs. At fourteen, she was on her knees praying to God to spare her from marrying. She was determined to secure her own right to independence but closed her mind to the matter of women's rights.

There were new developments in the oil business that seemed more important.

CHAPTER FOUR

The Birth of the Octopus

*I*N CLEVELAND, OHIO, in 1855, John Davison Rockefeller had begun his career as a bookkeeper in the wholesale grocery business at the age of sixteen, earning twenty-five dollars a month. He educated himself by keeping his ears open and soon had a partnership of his own. The son of a con man who occasionally posed as a deaf-mute peddler or a doctor offering miracle cures, young Rockefeller cultivated startling personal discipline, determination, religious conviction, and ambition. Acquiring money did not encourage self-indulgence but was rather a means of achieving strict control over his life, for he was a churchgoing family man who spent evenings at home. He claimed later that he learned the principles of business from his father, who was "involved in different enterprises." While the elder Rockefeller was neither principled nor businesslike, he apparently passed on to his son a willingness to take great risks when others didn't dare.

From his long-suffering mother, John D. Rockefeller acquired piety and the belief that God was guiding his course. In return, he

John D. Rockefeller in his early twenties.

contributed a tithe, or tenth, of his growing income to his church, humbly
volunteering to sweep the church floor. Secure in his own superior virtue,
Rockefeller was pugnaciously sensitive to the slights of men who thought
themselves better than he was. Once he got the upper hand over such rivals,
he would revel in sudden revenge.

In 1860 Rockefeller visited Titusville to see for himself what the new oil
business was all about. He traveled there in a train unpleasantly crowded
with raucous speculators, the overflow passengers clinging to the roofs of
the cars. On arrival he was appalled by the chaos and immorality infect-
ing the region. As for the oil that caused so much excitement, he observed,
"these vast stores of wealth were the gifts of the Great Creator." His belief

that oil was sent by heaven to relieve suffering mankind gave him the confidence to take big risks when the future looked bleak to his competitors. He combined "frugality and . . . prodigality — tight-fisted control of details and advocacy of unbridled expansion." He trolled the congregation of his church to find like-minded business associates. His unswerving (and self-serving) devotion to Baptist Christianity was the opposite of Ida's questioning of doctrine and her earnest efforts to form her own convictions. Even when Ida "went forward" to the rail at a revival meeting to show she was ready for salvation, an inner voice warned her that she was only doing so to be on the safe side.

After looking over Titusville, Rockefeller shifted his attention from groceries to oil. He discovered that refining oil to make it commercially useful involved little expense and produced high profits. With a colleague named Henry Flagler, Rockefeller founded the Standard and Excelsior Oil Works back in Cleveland, and his new business became an obsession. He often roused his brother William from sleep to tell him some new scheme that had come to him in the middle of the night.

Rockefeller was not alone in recognizing the potential fortune to be made in oil. Soon there were fifty refineries crowded together on the outskirts of Cleveland. Rockefeller and Flagler viewed competition among all the small oil producers as wasteful and immediately set out to absorb their rivals. By forcing them to sell out, Rockefeller and Flagler could make production more efficient and predictable.

The other key to dominating the oil business was control of its transport. Railroads had represented a huge opportunity for speculators during and after the Civil War. Track was laid on land deeded to investors by the government. Once the trains were running, owners reaped huge profits without having risked their own money. The wealth thus generated helped create a new class of businessmen known, for their ruthlessly arrogant methods, as robber barons. Growth and consolidation moved too fast for laws to keep up, even when legislators weren't bribed to look the other way.

The Erie, Central, and Pennsylvania Railroads all served the oil region, transporting oil to refineries, and their executives were quick to see that needless competition only wasted their resources. In 1871, the owners of these three railroads therefore presented Rockefeller with a scheme to eliminate competition. Rockefeller approved the plan and decided on the same goal for oil refining. The railroads would raise their oil freight rates by up to 250 percent and invite selected refiners to accept rebates, or partial repayment, not just on their own shipments but also on those of their competitors. The South Improvement Company (SIC) was created to enact the scheme. All refiners who signed on were pledged to absolute secrecy, as rebates were against the law.

———❋———

In early 1872, life was good for the Tarbells. Titusville prospered and spent money improving schools, churches, and cultural institutions. At four o'clock every afternoon, when weather permitted, the streets were cleared for a parade of the fast trotting horses belonging to the city's newly rich oil profiteers.

Five feet eight inches tall at fifteen, Ida towered over most women. She had long dark wavy hair and gray eyes with a clear, steady gaze enlivened by a mischievous twinkle. She was drafting a life plan, beginning with an outline and revising it as new ideas occurred to her. Having renounced truancy and returned to school — where she learned that her collecting hobby, so annoying to her mother, was actually science — she decided to become a biologist.

———❋———

When the railroad shipping rate increase went into effect, "suddenly this gay, prosperous town received a blow between the eyes." Men poured into the muddy streets of the oil region to compare rumors and vent their fury. In Titusville, three thousand men gathered at the Opera House. By now everyone was talking about a conspiracy engineered by the SIC. John Archbold, a young oil producer, took the stage and spoke about how he'd been approached by the SIC and refused to join it. Henry Rogers had also resisted its ploys and was elected secretary of the organization formed to fight back against it: the Petroleum Producers' Union.

The *Oil City Derrick* printed a list of conspirators; the name John D. Rockefeller leaped off it. Torchlit protests followed; the spectacle and the participants' outrage were seared in Ida's memory.

Ida relished the excitement of crisis, but the family paid a price at home. Her cheerful father stopped whistling, playing his harmonica, and relating the amusing experiences he'd had during the day. He and most of his fellow oil producers signed a pledge not to sell their product to Standard Oil in Cleveland. The embargo succeeded — for forty days the railroads received no freight from Oil City. Franklin even joined the mobs of vigilantes who actively opposed the SIC by wrecking its tank cars, along with those belonging to independents who cravenly went over to its side. He personally turned down Rockefeller's offer to buy a full year's output of oil. But the embargo's effect was short-lived.

Ida was studying the French Revolution in school, and the violence in Titusville seemed to her comparable to the fall of the Bastille. Titusville teachers and students alike sometimes left school to trade shares on the Oil Exchange, but to Ida's father, who had recently discouraged her from buying shares in an oil company, investing amounted to gambling. Franklin had no interest in understanding Rockefeller's strategy. He simply dismissed it as wrong.

Evangelical beliefs lay behind both Franklin's rejection of risk and Rockefeller's embrace of it. Rockefeller didn't consider business risk a gamble. His interpretation of Spencer's Social Darwinism was that Standard Oil had intervened and rescued the oil industry from a struggle for survival of the fittest, replacing it with "cooperation."

Franklin explained to Ida that railroads, like any other roads, existed to serve the public. Railroad owners had no right to issue special privileges to anyone. Ida wrote later, "In that fine fight [against the SIC], there was born in me a hatred of privilege—privilege of any sort. It was all pretty hazy, to be sure, but it still was well, at fifteen, to have one definite plan based on things seen and heard, ready for a future platform of social and economic justice if I should ever awake to my need of one." Legislators in Ohio

A riot during the oil wars of the early 1870s.

and Pennsylvania agreed with Franklin that railroads served the public and should charge equal rates. But no laws mandating this were passed for more than twenty years.

Meanwhile, the New York Petroleum Association, which had not been invited to join the SIC, sent a committee to Titusville to sound out the protesters who had successfully blocked all shipments of oil. The committee was headed by Henry Rogers, a former resident of Rouseville. Rogers quickly understood that if "South" were permitted to control the transportation of oil, it would put all the independents out of business. The railroads' owners, smarting from press reports that called them "villainous" and "robbers," abruptly capitulated. At a meeting with refiners on March 25, 1872, the railroad men conceded defeat, canceling the SIC contract. As the alleged leader of the conspiracy, Rockefeller was barred from entering the room by the oil men. The *New York Times* reporter on the scene described him as "looking pretty blue." The SIC ceased to exist. By this time, Rockefeller had absorbed twenty out of twenty-six refineries in the oil region. He continued to make secret deals with the railroads.

To Ida, Franklin personified the noble underdog. Just as she had idealized him as a "Paul Revere" figure, riding Flora home from Pithole, she now viewed him as the victim of malign forces. His heartfelt, if simplistic, ideas about fairness became the lens through which she viewed the triumph of combination (corporate) business in America and its terrible human cost.

"In walking through the world there is a choice for a man to make," Ida wrote later. "He can choose the fair and open path, the path which sound ethics, sound democracy and the common law prescribe, or choose the secret way by which he can get the better of his fellow man. It was that choice made by powerful men that suddenly confronted the Oil Region. The sly, secret greedy way won in the end, and bitterness and unhappiness and incalculable ethical deterioration for the country at large came out of that struggle and others like it which were going on all over the country — an old struggle."

As president of the National Refiners' Association, Rockefeller made overtures to independent refiners, promising to control prices and prevent overproduction. Cooperation, not competition, was his byword. By 1868, Rockefeller owned the largest refinery in the world. By 1877, he controlled 90 percent of the nation's oil production. In 1882, he established the Standard Oil Trust, a new kind of business organization designed to ensure a monopoly and fix, or determine, prices. Those who succumbed to his wily appeals were given stock in what was becoming an unprecedented industrial giant. Franklin, true to his principles to the last, refused to join up and struggled financially for the rest of his life.

CHAPTER FIVE

An Education

$\mathcal{E}$STHER WAS DETERMINED that her daughter receive an education. Both parents had taught Ida that life must have a purpose. The purpose she chose was to be a biologist, and the only way she'd be able to support herself was by teaching. Research facilities didn't hire women, nor was an independent career feasible. As had become her habit, she revised her life plan to accommodate her ambition. Few young women went to college in the 1870s. Coeducation was in its infancy. Cornell University, a top school for science, had begun admitting women in 1872. Ida entered its name on her life plan.

Dr. Lucius Bugbee, the "delightful and entertaining" president of Allegheny College, came to the Tarbells' for dinner one Sunday in 1876. When Ida told him her plan, he immediately put in a word for his own school. The Civil War had caused a slump in the college's enrollment as young men left to join the Union army. To compensate, the college began to recruit young women, over trustees' objections. Bugbee pointed out to Ida that Allegheny had begun accepting women earlier than Cornell.

Lucius Bugbee in 1880.

The president's attention was flattering, but Ida could resist flattery. More effectively, Bugbee aroused her sense of fairness. She felt a responsibility to "prove that women wanted a college education by supporting those colleges in their vicinity." Allegheny was only thirty miles from Titusville. There were few other female candidates in Allegheny's geographic area, so she felt it was up to her to be a pioneer. When she arrived at the college in September 1876, she was the lone female in her class, and there were only four others in the classes ahead of her.

Dedicated to learning, upholding hallowed traditions, Allegheny College was modeled after venerable intellectual centers in the East. The green-lawned campus was a world apart from Titusville and the ramshackle oil towns. Ida thought Bentley Hall, built in 1815 and the oldest building at Allegheny, the most beautiful structure she had ever seen.

The girls' dormitory wasn't ready for occupancy, so Ida boarded with President Bugbee's family, a situation that exposed her bashfulness to a painful degree. "I could have gone anywhere with less suffering," she recalled later. She must have presented a picture of extreme self-conscious misery. After a week she was moved to another faculty home.

The staff member responsible for the care and comfort of the coeds said she was "Lost in the Wilderness of Boy." The undergraduate men harshly resented coeducation. It was commonly believed that women's brains, smaller than men's (the missing five ounces, the difference in the weight of male and female brains, were frequently cited), were inadequate to handle demanding academic work. Courses would have to be simplified for them, underserving everyone else. Male "experts" asserted that education was dangerous for women, who had been selected by evolution for their tenderness, intuition, and domestic capabilities, while men were selected for courage and intellect. The differences were permanent. The birthrate among educated women had been declining. In response, magazines published articles warning that vigorous thought warped young girls' emotional and reproductive powers.

Bentley Hall.

Educationally, the gap between men and women was nowhere more evident than in science. Stanford University's president proclaimed that females would reduce the study of science to sentimentalism: "There would be nothing ruggedly true, ruggedly masculine left in it." It was painful for Ida to absorb such resentment. It didn't help that she sympathized with the desire of Allegheny's men to be left alone.

Ida experienced other humiliations, such as having to wear many layers of awkward clothing to combat the terrible cold or, in warmer weather, hoop skirts that were unmanageable in crowds or wind, causing "one crisis after another." Boys would gather at intersections for glimpses of leg. Girls "minced down the street with padded bustles thrust out behind, padded busts thrust out in front, their heads held [as] far back as nature would allow," an exercise called "the Grecian bend." Ida later laughed at herself for following suit.

In time, more girls arrived, which bolstered the confidence of the "pioneers," and the relationships between the sexes began to improve. For Ida, it took a while. Her dread of marriage meant avoidance of romance, which in turn meant tiptoeing around the opposite sex. She was extremely shy and by her own reckoning, immature. Still, she'd had easy relationships with her father's and brother's friends in Titusville, even though Methodism forbade dancing and she was no good at games.

Over the years at Allegheny, Ida lived in three different dormitories set up for the increasing number of girls who entered the school. The first was a little house with seven or eight rooms called Snow Flake. It sat next to a boys' dorm, inviting practical jokes and flirtation. But these antics were kept to a minimum, as the girls were conscious that any misbehavior threatened the experiment of coeducation. Female students had a ten p.m. curfew, but violations weren't punished. One year, Ida lived on the first floor of the girls' dormitory, and curfew breakers crawled in through her window. The boys at Allegheny slept two to a bed. Ida probably shared her room and her bed as well.

She usually had a male escort for occasions that called for one, such as fifty-cent chicken dinners off campus and bobsledding parties. The latter meant riding under warm robes, when a boy might ease his arm around a girl's waist. A good-night kiss was "a dangerous feat." Four fraternity men separately offered Ida their pins, and, not wanting to disappoint anyone, she accepted them all. When she wore them to chapel affixed in a row on her bosom, there were ruffled feelings.

Ida was never ambivalent about learning. She studied English literature, philology, French, Latin, German, art history, and the sciences. Her greatest passions were awakened in the science lab. She decided it was a good thing she hadn't gone to Cornell, for Allegheny's Professor Jeremiah Tingley, in-tense yet approachable, was the perfect mentor. He had been chosen to study with Louis Agassiz, America's foremost scien-tist, and shared Agassiz's faith in nature's eternal truths. (Agassiz, who was generally revered, was an evolution denier.) Ida ad-opted Tingley's pantheism, which placed God in nature, and his scientific method of observation and classification, summed up by the injunction "Look inside." The sur-face of a thing told nothing, Tingley said. It must be taken apart to be truly examined. This is how Ida would practice investigative journalism later on.

Professor Jeremiah Tingley.

Tingley gave his serious students the run of his laboratory, which, along with old furniture and janitorial supplies, was consigned to a basement. He urged Ida to put received knowledge aside and examine phenomena for herself, in particular through his binocular microscope. When Ida told him she was interested in evolution, he assigned her a one-lunged local mud-puppy (a kind of salamander), about a foot long, to dissect. It was supposed to represent a "missing link" between earliest water- and land-based creatures. The thing was "slimy" and "loathsome," but Ida felt privileged to be allowed to study it on her own, as if she were already a real scientist.

It was an era of prolific inventing, and Professor Tingley kept up with the latest marvels. When Franklin attended the spectacular 1876 Centennial Exhibition in Philadelphia, where the telephone was demonstrated, Ida was released from classes to go with him. Afterward, Tingley rigged up a phone in the Allegheny lab and demonstrated it for the students. "Some day you'll talk to your homes from these rooms," he said. "New York will talk to Boston!" What a contrast his enthusiasm was to her father's rigid skepticism! Franklin had scoffed when a Bell Company agent tried to sell him stock in the brand-new telephone company. Ida was most impressed, not by the instrument and its amazing potential, but by Tingley's optimism. She had been raised in a world of dogged puritans afraid to show enthusiasm, never passionate about their work. That was what she wanted for herself: the excitement and joy of work with a purpose.

Ida's Latin professor, George Haskins, heaped scorn on his students when they failed to grasp the rich history and importance of the language. Haskins's contempt for slackers shocked Ida, but she reformed with a vengeance, just as she had after being rebuked by Mrs. French in Titusville. One of her friends remembered that Ida got up at four a.m. to study and demanded perfection of herself, yet insisted Ida was not a grind, or relentless studier. "She was too interested in people." The friend recalled that when Will followed Ida to Allegheny, his sister advised him not to join a fraternity so that he would be exposed to a wider circle of acquaintances.

Ida earned a reputation for being fearless, fun loving, and a natural leader. She wore skirts that showed her ankles, shocking some conservative types. When she skipped across a puddle, her scarlet petticoat showed.

Her formal classes in literature and composition were, unfortu-

William Tarbell as a college student.

nately, "meagre." Looking back, she wished that Professor Tingley's methods had been applied to them, which would have taught her that "the matter of writing lies first in what Montaigne calls 'clear and lively images.' . . . To look within yourself, to find your own thought about a thing, your own feelings about a thing, and then get that down with all the art you can command, and with a consciousness you can grow in that art." College courses didn't teach her that. She came by the insight only after years of perfecting her craft as a writer.

She joined the student newspaper and the all-female Ossoli Society, named for Margaret Fuller Ossoli, America's most brilliant woman of letters. Its members composed essays, debated, and lectured. Ida was awarded a prize for one of her talks. At their parties, some of the Ossolis dressed as

The editorial staff of the Allegheny student newspaper. Ida is seated in the chair at center.

men, an innocent way of playing with power. Ida appropriated her brother's military uniform and admired the way she looked in it.

Her sophomore class wanted to leave a monument of some kind to the school but lacked funds. Someone thought of a stone, so they managed, with the help of an engineering student, to move a boulder about the size of a small stuffed chair to a suitable high spot on campus. Ida spearheaded the selection of an inscription, which showed the influence of Professor Tingley: *Spes sibi quisque,* "Your hope lies within."

Rising at four a.m. to study may have taken its toll. In her senior year, Ida was given permission to study at home and was urged to take the semester off because of her health. She managed to complete her courses. The title of her senior oration was "The Work of Novels." She praised Dickens's complex characters based upon human nature and dismissed romantic fiction as "a grotesque collection of fallacies." She graduated on time with her class.

Though Ida entered Allegheny determined never to marry, she left it feeling not so sure about that. The vow she had made at fourteen had been softened by mutual respect and enjoyment among the undergraduate men and women. An anonymous note on a class photograph in the college archives identifies a young male as "engaged to Ida M. Tarbell — neither married." Ten years later, Ida wrote a poem recalling moonlit talks with a man about women's obligations and rights, but she graduated without a fiancé or any compelling attachment. Her ambition was to study in Europe with a great scientist. There was no such opportunity for a woman in America.

At the time, for a career other than teaching, a genteel, educated, and adventure-seeking Methodist woman could do missionary work in Asia or Africa. Church elders tried to recruit Ida, insisting she had a "calling to serve God." Instead, she applied for a job at the Poland Union Seminary, a school in Poland, Ohio. Lengthy negotiations, during which Ida triumphed over a candidate with twenty years of teaching experience, produced the offer of an annual salary of five hundred dollars. Ida was replacing the long-beloved preceptress, or head of school, who had departed when her pay was cut, leaving her students indignant. Ida didn't know that history, and the job seemed almost too good to be true. She was joining the ranks of newly minted career women. Since teaching couldn't possibly use up all her time at the seminary, she expected to devote free hours to research with her microscope.

CHAPTER SIX

A Job and a Calling

*I*DA ARRIVED IN the pleasant town of Poland the following August in an innocent state of mind. "If I had been going on my honeymoon," she wrote later, "I should scarcely have been more expectant or more curious."

Laid out by its eighteenth-century founders from Connecticut, Poland had a storybook appeal. Admiring the tidy architecture as she strolled the streets, Ida was accosted by citizens who were upset by her predecessor's departure. Their unexpected resentment threw her off balance and made her feel guilty. Moreover, she was given a staggering teaching schedule at the seminary: two classes each in French, German, Greek, and Latin; as well as geology, botany, geometry, and trigonometry! She found it was possible to keep barely ahead of the students by cramming late every night.

When Ida's morale was lowest, a young woman introduced herself. Her friendship would make Ida's stay in Poland "in many ways the happiest of [her] life up to that time." The daughter of a trustee, Clara Walker, called Dot, was "a fine example of the out-of-doors girl of the

This grand house in picturesque Poland, Ohio, belonged to the Walker family. Dot Walker was Ida's good friend.

1880s," the girl who had revolted against laced-up corsets, high heels, long skirts. She had "direct, merry eyes that looked upon and saw everything." Ida was instantly charmed. Here was a spirited, energetic, uninhibited, open-minded girl with very modern flair.

Dot whisked Ida off for a buggy ride to fill her in on the local scene. The countryside was being industrialized, bringing an influx of unassimilated immigrant labor. Dot was as concerned with "unfairness" as Ida was, and knew where it existed. In Ida she found an eager pupil with everything to learn.

On lovely farmland, Dot pointed out mines newly dug to feed the hungry furnaces of industry, with squalid housing for workers nearby. The local

This group photo includes Dot, standing on the right, and Ida, seated at left.

economy and its timeless way of life were surrendering to progress. Men and women were doing punishing work for a new class of industrialists who were growing rich by exploiting natural resources and creating giant business "combinations." Ida saw the unprecedented problems of the modern age in microcosm: "The destruction of beauty, the breaking down of the standards of conduct, the love of money for money's sake, the grist of social problems facing the countryside from the inflow of foreigners and the instability of work."

One day she and Dot watched, horrified, as carts laden with charred bodies crossed their path. A smelting furnace had exploded. Ida was even more unstrung by the spectacle of a mob of women rioting to protest a plant closing. This was her first intimation that women were not all peaceful by nature.

Ida had never seen this kind of working-class suffering up so close. She realized that the desperate plight of the industrial poor could not be remedied by the simple charity her parents had practiced, handing out food or coffee to vagrants at their back door. Providing meaningful help was too much even for organized religion to manage.

Dot Walker's encouragement helped Ida maintain her sanity when she had to lead a group of district schoolteachers through a short annual refresher course called Verb Grammar and Percentage Math. The class mattered because the seminary depended on the teachers' tuition payments. The district teachers were older than Ida and openly hostile toward her. The course included sets of trick questions meant to test comprehension. The district teachers spouted correct answers instantly and sniggered when Ida struggled to figure out the logic behind these ready responses. She often woke up in the middle of the night in a cold sweat, dreading the following day's confrontation with people who thought her too inexperienced for her post. In time, she realized they had memorized the answers from a book. Ida made up new questions and demanded that the class figure out the answers for themselves. The teachers balked at first, but she managed to persuade them that learning useful principles was better than parroting answers without understanding them.

Ida left the Poland Union Seminary by mutual agreement after two years. She had grown as a person, but her prospects for a life in science weren't much better than they had been two years before. Biology was still a male preserve. Her father had paid her college tuition, but financial support for graduate study was out of the question. She hadn't saved money; in fact, she had borrowed from her father when she couldn't stretch her salary to cover expenses.

So Ida went home to Titusville. She set up her microscope in the tower room again and launched a study of *Hydrozoa,* small fresh- and saltwater creatures, of which the hydra is the best known. Allegheny College offered her a job teaching French and German, but she was not at all tempted. She was all taught out and in "retreat." She had suffered a setback. Home was a sanctuary but offered little independence from her hovering family.

In 1882, after Ida had been home for a few months, the Reverend Theodore Flood came to Titusville to preach, and Esther Tarbell invited him to dinner.

Ida at home in Titusville.

Flood was editing a journal published by the Chautauqua movement, a regular summer series of lectures and courses designed to bring higher education home to America's middle class. A few years before, John Heyl Vincent, a Methodist minister, had been asked by Chautauqua's president to set up an institute that would connect students of Chautauqua courses of study with the main currents of contemporary culture. Ida had been present at the summer session in 1878 when Vincent announced the home study course that would be comparable to four years of college, costing five dollars a year including books and requiring an average of forty minutes' reading per day. He called it the Chautauqua Literary and Scientific Circle. Ida saw its value for women: "Women's desire for knowledge had been intensified by the Women's Rights movement, in which the strongest plank had been a demand . . . for higher education." Vincent had founded the *Chautauquan,* a magazine that published supplements to the course readings.

On the night when Flood came to dinner and learned that Ida was unemployed, he realized that her college degree and multidisciplinary teaching experience could solve a problem for the magazine. Many of the articles contained material that confused readers who didn't own reference books, and the magazine's mailbox overflowed with queries from these puzzled patrons. Ida was someone who could anticipate such questions and write explanatory marginal notes where they were needed. Flood offered her a sample article to annotate. It was fun. Ida delighted in what she knew and loved even more finding out what she didn't, although she worried that she might make a mistake and mislead a subscriber. She passed the test handily.

Once officially hired, she moved to Meadville, the magazine's headquarters, so that she could consult her beloved Allegheny College library. She lived first with the Floods, then in her own rented room, and finally with three self-reliant colleagues in an arrangement recommended by feminist Mary Livermore. They shared food preparation, hired cleaning and washing help, kept common accounts, and talked shop over dinner.

Ida began as Flood's "girl Friday" and quickly became indispensable,

The Reverend Theodore Flood.

learning every aspect of magazine publication and even apprenticing herself to the foreman of the printing shop. She prepared each issue, from editing manuscripts with a blue pencil to making paste-ups to proofreading galleys. The office, first in Flood's home, later in modern quarters equipped with pneumatic tubes for communication between departments, was unusually friendly to women and their concerns. The masthead, or list of editors and contributors, was sprinkled with women's names. New editorial hires were often female. Clergymen and women cooperated in a sphere far removed from masculine preoccupation with expansion, bloody war, and building wealth.

The Chautauqua self-help movement offered instruction in music, art, and literature as well as information about new technologies, social problems, foreign affairs, manners, and even hygiene. It grew exponentially while Ida was attached to it, becoming "a virtually official middle class image of America." Its adherents could firmly distinguish themselves from the "lavish and conspicuous squandering of wealth among the very rich and the squalor of the very poor."

In her later years Ida spoke of "great revolts" in her girlhood, the "forgotten battles [labor versus management] of the 1880s," and the "terrible tension between making life easier for many while bringing enormous poverty, concentrating greater wealth in just a few hands." In the 1885 novel *The Rise of Silas Lapham* by William Dean Howells, money is referred to as the romance, the poetry of the age. That period was dubbed the Gilded Age by Mark Twain. It represented a huge shift in American values. Before money loomed so large, social and political problems had seemed manageable; they could be addressed by the pious and the charitable in communities. Now these issues dwarfed the individual, and addressing them seemed beyond the powers even of churches and larger philanthropies.

Ida read the *New York Tribune* every day at the office, following the stories of strikes and their violent suppression. Factory workers had been staging wildcat strikes since the late eighteenth century. The long depression that began in the 1870s resulted in strikes organized by early unions in the coal, copper, steel, and railroad industries and retaliation by management. The unrest involved immigrants with "European" (Marxist) ideas that posed to some the threat of class struggle in America. The response of the industrialists was often extreme. "If the master race of this continent is subordinated to or overrun with the communistic or revolutionary races, it will be in grave danger of social disaster," thundered an editorial, echoing the Social Darwinist view that fitter Anglo-Saxon American men had a right to America's resources.

The new mass of unskilled laborers that began arriving in the 1880s had much less hope of rising in the world than earlier artisans and mechanics had. Their only power to improve their lot seemed to lie in the strike. In Wyoming in 1885, white miners and railroad workers murdered the Chinese who had been hired to replace them at lower wages. Armies of the millions of unemployed roamed the countryside, looking for work. Harvard's president organized a student militia to defend its property. Vigilante law-and-order leagues were formed in many communities, and cities built imposing armories. A journalist wrote in 1877, "It seemed as if the whole social and political structure was on the very brink of ruin."

Ida urged Flood to have the *Chautauquan* cover the pressing needs behind the unrest: a workday limited to eight hours, temperance, and improved conditions in the immigrant-filled slums. He agreed, but the magazine's benign, optimistic approach wasn't adequate to report, much less analyze, the turmoil that roiled American life. Mechanization was replacing craft, cities were sucking populations from the countryside, a class hierarchy from rich to poor was supplanting republican egalitarianism. Railroad timetables were forcing people to live by the clock, adding to the stress of daily life. Chautauqua was designed to reassure the middle class and make its members feel they met their responsibilities to society simply by being informed. Ida chafed at this soothing purpose.

As small businesses succumbed to hard times, John D. Rockefeller was busy seizing the opportunity to absorb them cheaply. Standard Oil became known as "the octopus" because of its long reach into every aspect of the oil business. Mothers in the oil region warned their fidgety children to be quiet and go to sleep, or Rockefeller would get them.

Standard Oil's domination of the market directly threatened Franklin Tarbell's investments in oil wells. In 1882, after losing money steadily, he and Will decided to try their luck in Dakota Territory, where railroads were promoting wheat farming. The story handed down in the Tarbell family was that Franklin gave up the plan when the prairie winds blew off his toupee. Will stayed for a while, met a young woman named Ella Scott, and married her.

Ida was feeling some ambivalence about her own professional life. On her twenty-eighth birthday, in 1885, she confided to her journal, "For the first time in my life I am beginning to doubt the blessing that I have always claimed lay in work. It has stifled my impatience, kept me steady, acted as an opiate. But now leisure — golden leisure to think, to expand, to flourish. I wonder if this is a step in mental development. I perhaps could not have appreciated leisure without first loving work."

In another entry, she wrote: "Will I succeed? Victory resides in Will."

In addition to her work for the magazine, Ida was jotting scenes, moral reflections, character studies, odd and amusing occurrences, and quotations from other writers in a little notebook.

> The Trail of the serpent . . . schoolgirl commits suicide . . . betrayed by a married man . . . a man ditto can't get work . . . a one-armed boy — carelessness of father — a sick servant — carelessness of the mistress . . . a woman was denied by her husband the new things she wanted for her house and in retaliation she put up a placard in the window: poor but respectable . . . Teacher: "Do you love Jesus?" Boy: "No. But I got nuthin' agin him."

She satirized the new business trusts:

> All commodities will be centered in trusts — not just oil and sugar but eye glasses, shrimp salad and pate de foie gras. Each in the hands of say five persons . . . a set of families with common interest. Let us call it an order — Order of Oyster, Olive, Poultry.

She also composed poems and musings on the subject of love. She abandoned fragments like these before they could be developed into stories, a revealing sign of creative and emotional restlessness in search of an outlet.

Ida also took practical steps to fulfill herself. "Having convinced [her] editor-in-chief that [she] could keep his house in better order than he had been interested in doing," she began writing for the magazine. Although seeing her words in stark print made her nervous, it was more gratifying than anything else she'd done. The December 1886 issue was a watershed for Ida, marking the start of her new confidence. It ran her first signed article.

The article, "The Arts and Industries of Cincinnati," was typical of the magazine, a fact-filled portrait of an American city. After praising some of the city's cultural institutions, she remarked, "Morally, Cincinnati has much

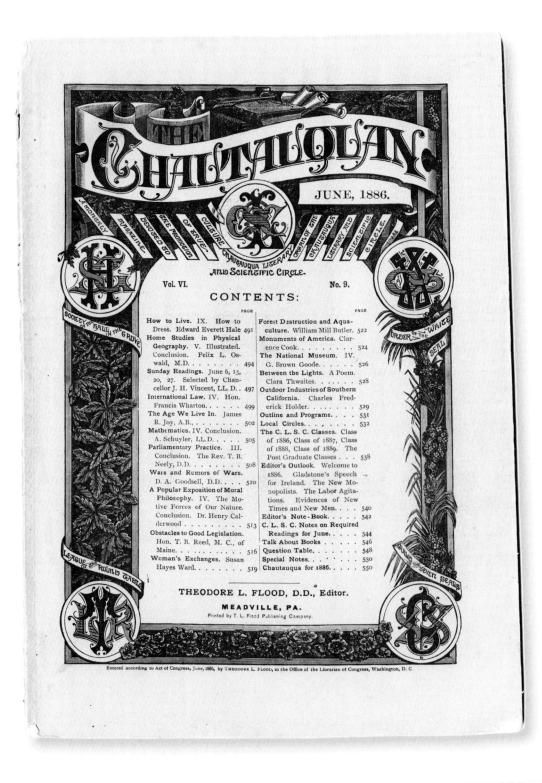

THE CHAUTAUQUAN

JUNE, 1886.

A MONTHLY MAGAZINE DEVOTED TO THE PROMOTION OF TRUE CULTURE. ORGAN OF THE CHAUTAUQUA LITERARY AND SCIENTIFIC CIRCLE.

Vol. VI.   **No. 9.**

CONTENTS:

THEODORE L. FLOOD, D.D., Editor.

MEADVILLE, PA.

Printed by T. L. Flood Publishing Company.

Cover of the Chautauquan, *June 1886.*

to learn." Lucid and enlivened by brisk indignation, the story was a harbinger of her mature style.

Her next article, "Women as Inventors," published in 1887, challenged an earlier piece that had run in the magazine. The woman writer had claimed that because of male domination, American women had produced only three hundred patented inventions—compared to tens of thousands by men—and those mostly for domestic devices. Ida was always irritated by women's special pleading; in this case, instinct told her that the article wasn't backed up by facts and that women's real achievements were being discounted to make a point. "I had been disturbed for some time by what seemed to me the calculated belittling of the past achievements of women by many active in the suffrage campaign," she reported later.

True to her scientific training, she went to Washington to examine the Patent Office records and found that more than two thousand patents had been issued to women. The fact that many of them were indeed for domestic devices didn't diminish the achievement. "Power to create breaks all barriers," she confidently contended. "Women had demonstrated this again and again while carrying on what I, as an observer of society was coming to regard as the most delicate, complex, essential of all creative tasks—the making of a home." Ida's fierce attachment to home—both her own family home and the abstract idea of home as a sacred and regenerative place—had become political.

After the magazine published an article recommending that women pursue careers in journalism because they could then examine and write about progressive subjects, Ida produced her own essay titled "Women in Journalism" in April 1887. It has a remarkably authoritative tone for one whose career was still in the formative stage. To would-be journalists, she stressed the crucial importance of accuracy for credibility, of getting a broad education, and of being willing to work very hard. While a woman could succeed in journalism, Ida noted, "she must not put forward her femininity to such an extent as to demand that the habits of the office be changed on her account; nor can she presume on her womanhood."

Years later, in a piece called "The Disillusionment of Women," Ida confessed her dislike of "going where I wasn't wanted," adding that she had "a certain skill in getting what I wanted by another route." To her, openly demanding equal treatment represented special pleading and therefore an admission that women's gifts weren't equal to men's.

Ida thought women had an inborn sensitivity to the need for moral reform. Women journalists were especially qualified to focus on "large opportunities for doing good, for influencing public opinion, and for purifying the atmosphere of the times." She observed that what passed for objective journalism was filled with errors and distortions, and women writers were equipped to correct them: "There is not a single missionary field upon which a woman can enter that is more promising or more important than that of establishing among plain people the habit of thinking clearly and soundly on the one thousand and one questions on which they are forced to give their opinion, either directly or indirectly by their vote." In other words, women — who weren't allowed to vote — might positively influence the votes of men.

The question of how women could best inspire reform set Ida to thinking about the oil wars of her childhood. They had been waged in a man's world, which women like her mother had struggled to civilize. She began making notes for a novel that would trace the rise of oil, with its great potential for good and the bitter conflicts it had caused. What, she asked herself, was woman's place in this man-made, man-run world? Although she couldn't seem to sustain the writing of fiction and abandoned the project, the question stayed with her.

Staff of the Chautauquan, *1888. Ida is at left.*

The society that had formed her, when women had been content to be the civilizing force, was being challenged by a new generation of women who wanted full civil rights to property, jobs, divorce, and, most important, the vote. Women had never participated in American government. How would they use civil rights if they got them?

Ida believed that no problem of the present could be solved until people understood how that problem had been handled in the past. She felt that the French Revolution had lessons for her time. It had produced several political heroines. Ida was fluent enough in French to translate general-interest articles from the French periodical *Revue des deux mondes* for the *Chautauquan*. After reading as many books as she could find, she wrote profiles of Madame de Staël, mistress of a famous salon, or gathering of conversationalists; Marie Antoinette, queen of France; and Madame Roland, a learned woman who fought alongside her husband for liberty and was guillotined by the followers of Robespierre. In her last days in prison, Roland had composed her memoirs and defined the role that women should play in a republic. Ida was fascinated by Roland and hoped one day to write a book about her.

In the meantime, she published a piece of short fiction called "Why Women Are Restless." In it, a housewife flees her home because money is doled out to her a nickel at a time, a plight similar to Esther's. Ida's sympathies lay not with the restless homemaker but rather with the unappreciated working woman. The ungrateful homemaker didn't "know what it means to those who are living hand to hand . . . to escape into a home of their own and hear the door shut behind them."

————— ※ —————

After six years on the *Chautauquan,* Ida worried that her intellect might no longer be developing. As managing editor she handled one subject after another, never pursuing anything very far. The magazine gobbled everything she wrote. She had no sustained work of her own, nothing she could pursue to its depths. Reverend Flood's domain exuded contentment with things as they were. So did the Chautauqua Institution on the lake. The philosopher William James wrote of his stay there: "I long to escape from tepidity . . . a change from the blamelessness of Chautauqua as she lies soaking in the year after year lakeside sun and showers. Man wants to be stretched to his utmost." And upon leaving: "Ouf, what a relief! Now for something

Socializing on the grounds of the Chautauqua Institution.

primordial and savage . . . to set the balance straight again. This order is too tame, this culture second-rate, this goodness too uninspiring." He found Chautauqua's disinfected culture "effeminate, devoid of opportunities for manly heroism."

Ida continued to harbor similar thoughts. "The tumults, the challenges of my day had finally penetrated my aloofness, and . . . I was feeling more and more the need to take a part in them." Why avoid the straitjacket of marriage only to be numbed by her job? She must have felt taken for granted in a wifely way by Flood. Outside the office, the citizens of Meadville wanted above all to preserve their comforts. One Sunday, her preacher confronted the congregation with the cry: "You're dyin' of respectability!" Always taking a thought at least one step further, Ida reflected that too much destructive change had occurred in her lifetime for her to count on security. She had risen as far as she could on the magazine and would have to accept its limitations if she stayed — but Ida could not accept limitations.

Those women of the French Revolution still called to her, especially Madame Roland. Ida admired clear, concise French prose and the way history was presented in France to a popular audience. To write her book, Ida would have to move to Paris to do research.

To live in Paris! The idea was exciting, terrifying. How would she survive?

Instead of hiring reporters and writers, American newspapers filled their pages with general-interest articles purchased from syndicates. Could Ida support herself by sending such pieces from Paris? She eagerly tackled this new possibility, traveling to Cincinnati, Pittsburgh, and other cities, meeting with editors and persuading half a dozen to take future articles at six dollars each. On this slim promise, she resigned from the *Chautauquan* and later described the ensuing discussion:

"Flood said, 'How will you support yourself?'

"'By writing.'

"'You're not a writer. You'll starve.'

"He had touched the weakest point in my venture: I was not a writer and I knew it."

She knew only that she wasn't a poet or a novelist; she *had* become a journalist. "It was my sense of what mattered, and not somebody else's, that would give my work freshness and strength."

It was a huge gamble. Friends said she was crazy. Nevertheless, two of her colleagues at the magazine, Mary Henry and Jo Henderson, were so impressed by her gumption that they quit at the same time to go with her to Paris on extended holidays. Flood wrote a letter of recommendation to potential employers indicating that Ida was leaving for reasons of health. She harbored a deep resentment of him for years afterward, but there is no

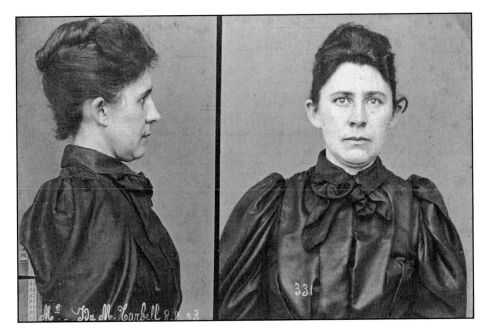

Ida's passport photos.

record of exactly why, beyond his contemptuous "You'll starve!" In a letter home she referred to her "beheading in Meadville." She warned her family against retaliation, but at the same time urged Will to work quietly against Flood, who had decided to run for Congress in 1891. "I don't care if he does go to Congress . . . he is one of those men who don't need to be helped to destruction. He's bound to kill himself unless, indeed, he sees the evil of his ways."

In Titusville, Ida spent three afternoons a week with a Frenchman until she was fluent in everyday conversation. She was embarking for the first time upon a course she had set entirely by herself. "I wanted freedom," she wrote. She was thirty-three. In those days, that meant past her prime, an old maid. For Ida it was a thrilling new beginning.

CHAPTER SEVEN

Paris

THE CHAPTER ON the Paris years in Ida's memoir is titled "I Fall in Love." She adored Paris. Her affair with the city kept her from despairing even when she didn't have enough to eat. She was removed from the troubling changes taking place in America. (Europe was changing too, but beneath a "thousand thicknesses of tradition," as Henry James put it.) And she loved the French, loved that they were not restless like her countrymen.

From the day she sailed for France, in early August 1891, Ida kept up a stream of breezy, entertaining letters to her family. She reported on the layout of the ship, on her fellow passengers, and on her seasickness. ("I have become a clam. The evolution has been sudden and complete and necessary. It is that — or a basin.") She reported excitedly on everything, with artfully chosen details meant to inform and amuse. She wanted them to see for themselves: "You must come over. Sell your silver. Sell your overcoats, sell *anything* and *everything* but come to Europe." She assured them that "the people are not vicious. I never saw a city full of such decent-looking people." Most of her letters were addressed to the family group, but occasionally she wrote to them individually. She addressed her brother, Will, ironically as "my sweetheart" and referred to herself as his "lady love."

She had determined that the cheapest lodgings, convenient to the university, were to be found on the Left Bank of the Seine, where many artists and intellectuals lived. Ida was in charge of arrangements; her friends followed her lead, even referring to her as *Maman,* French for "Mama."

She began writing the articles that would be her bread and butter, describing her experiences of improvising and economizing as she and her friends set up a household in a foreign city. In a piece on safety, she noted that in Paris women could dine alone in restaurants without incurring disapproval. Though chronically strapped for funds, she and her friends found life to be filled with rich offerings. They were uplifted by the novelty of everything they saw and did. Lack of money never prevented Ida from entertaining callers, seeing the sights, or being welcomed into French intellectual society.

It took her six anxious weeks to make her first sale — one article for six dollars. Of this small triumph she remarked with lingering bitterness that Flood would "scorn it." She kept her expenses to fifty cents a day.

Over the next few months, Ida began to establish a reputation. The *Pittsburgh Dispatch* published an endorsement with the piece she sent them: "From what we know of Miss Tarbell, she is bound to make a place for herself in American literature." Heady stuff! Inspired by her romantic surroundings, she took a stab at writing a short story set in France. With a mix of apprehension and pride, she sent it off to *Scribner's Magazine,* a literary beacon. Was she reaching too high? She tried not to think about it while awaiting a reply.

At the Sorbonne, Paris's great university, she observed, "The people come and go as they please absolutely." When latecomers entered lecture halls, the other students stomped and cheered. "They don't dislike women students but they jeer them," she added. She attended lectures on historiography among students who, she judged, were not much younger than she.

Her landlady rented rooms to a gaggle of aristocratic young Egyptian students, all males, who were adorably susceptible to the frank American girls. There was a good deal of silliness in their socializing and exchanges of information about courtship and marriage in the two cultures. The Egyptians loved games and charades and behaved, Ida said, like delightful children. Their talk could be serious as well, and the young men were far more worldly than the American girls. Ida had conquered, or outgrown, her shyness with the opposite sex, and she assured her family that all encounters were conducted with propriety.

Charles Downer Hazen.

A group of students and faculty from Johns Hopkins provided even more agreeable company for sightseeing and trading witty observations while they lingered over small plates at little restaurants. Ida and Charles Downer Hazen, who was ten years younger and several inches shorter than she, found a special rapport in the easy candor of their exchanges and their mutual literary ambitions. She referred to him in her letters as her roommate Mary Henry's particular friend, not her own. But she and Hazen sat talking in cafés for hours — almost too conspicuously, according

The Moulin Rouge nightclub.

to another friend, who was probably teasing them. Hazen, studying history, was an excellent sounding board for Ida's ideas about Madame Roland. At some point they made the happy discovery that both were determined to avoid marriage.

Boldly, they ventured to the Moulin Rouge, a nightclub featuring scantily clad cancan dancers. "But here goes—I have been to see the can-can," she told her family. "When I get home I'll tell you what I saw. I don't like to write it." She advised them to read Mark Twain's description if they were curious. In *The Innocents Abroad,* published in 1869, he had written: "That is the Can-can. The idea of it is to dance as wildly, as noisily, as furiously as you can; expose yourself as much as possible if you are a woman; and kick as high as you can, no matter which sex you belong to."

Ida wasn't spared bad news from Titusville. Despairing over Standard Oil's stranglehold on independent oil producers, her father's partner committed suicide, leaving Franklin saddled with debts. Will wrote to her about the independent refiners that were failing and informed her that a lawsuit had forced minimal reorganization of Standard Oil in Ohio to comply with regulations, leaving it as powerful as ever. Will was determined to fight the octopus by organizing the independents.

Letters from home also told of sister Sarah's lingering illness and Esther's many complaints about difficulties caused by family members and friends. It all made Ida feel helpless and guilty. How could she indulge herself in Paris while they suffered? Should she go home? But she hardened herself to the guilt through the first miserably cold winter. She and her roommates burned coal in a grate and wore layers and layers of clothes. Even so, there was no attraction yet in going home.

Then came an acceptance letter from *Scribner's*. The magazine would pay one hundred dollars for her short story — nearly as much as she had saved to come to Paris! Ida wept with joy. She *could* write! She wouldn't starve! She would stay two years. Now she paid close attention to the way older women on tiny fixed incomes seemed to manage, in case she found herself in that situation later in life. In America, poverty was a despised condition you were supposed to rise out of, while the French bore it with dignity. She watched a countess in threadbare clothing sift through garbage after dark. When this proud aristocrat visited a shop, its owner made a fuss and claimed to be honored by the visit, even if all the countess purchased was an egg. In Paris the worth of men and women was not measured by money.

Eager to master every trick of living like a native, Ida made herself known to the women who kept small shops in the neighborhood. When they pegged her as a *femme travailleuse,* a working woman, she was very pleased, even though the term carried the implication of "old maid."

She worked steadily, producing a stream of articles. She told her family she had wasted her first year but was now on track. A visiting American woman referred to Ida's revolt against security, meaning marriage. This woman concluded that in striking out on her own, Ida had hardened her heart toward the institution of the family. Ida considered the charge absurd, but it may have contributed to her defiant defense of hearth and home for women later on, as the suffrage movement gathered steam. A story she wrote in Paris depicted a struggle between a woman journalist, living a bohemian life, and a proper society matron who disapproves of her. The disapproval affects the journalist intensely. In the end, she marries, but not with any joy.

Ida's friends ended their extended vacation and sailed home in 1892, and she moved to much smaller quarters on the rue Malebranche, which had an iconic Parisian stairway. One day in June, a feeling of dread kept her from working. She fled her little room and walked the streets for hours. When she returned, *Le temps,* the afternoon newspaper, lay outside the door. Its headline made her knees buckle: TITUSVILLE WIPED OUT/CLOUDBURST, AWFUL FIRES, 150 KILLED.

Oil Creek had flooded, inflammable matter on its waters ignited, explosions resulted. Oily waters had poured in faster than a man could run. Half the town lay underwater. The event was compared to the Johnstown Flood, a Pennsylvania disaster that had taken place in 1889.

Ida waited in agony for word from home. Finally, hours later, her landlady handed her a telegram. It contained a single word: SAFE. Seeing this, Ida let out a shriek. A letter followed, confirming that the Tarbell house was standing and all its occupants were unharmed. The immense relief in the happy ending renewed Ida's energy. In her little room she wrote an article on the

Titusville, after the fire and flood of 1892.

paving of Paris streets and sent it to the newspaper syndicate founded by S. S. McClure. Soon afterward, a letter arrived from McClure himself. He was coming to Paris and wanted to meet her.

Days later in that summer of 1892, there was insistent knocking on her door. A man stood panting on the threshold, a watch in his hand and his pale, uncanny eyes fixed on her. He had run up four flights. "I've just ten minutes — must leave for Switzerland tonight!" he exclaimed in a high, clipped voice. It was Sam McClure.

He was thirty-five and no taller than Ida, slender, with a thatch of white-blond hair and a yellow mustache, a bewitching Irish lilt in his ebullient speech. He was nattily dressed and almost helplessly charming. At that moment his life seemed to depend on winning her over. Ida sat spellbound. She hadn't experienced such enthusiasm since the days in Professor Tingley's lab. The man was so disarming, she kept having to remind herself that this was indeed the famous S. S. McClure.

McClure put his watch away and seemed to forget all about the time while he told her his life story. He'd immigrated to America from Ireland as a small boy with his widowed mother and his brother, bitterly poor. Years later, he'd worked his way through Knox College in Galesburg, Illinois, selling pots and pans all over the Midwest (Ida wondered who could resist him). He'd sold microscopes, too. He had absorbed the spirit of Knox; founded by reformers and idealists, it had been a station on the Underground Railroad and the site of a Lincoln-Douglas debate. He had undertaken to memorize the meaning and derivation of every word in the English dictionary. He had seized control of the student newspaper and made it into a syndicate, selling articles to other college papers around the country. He'd fallen in love with a professor's beautiful, brainy daughter, had been forbidden to see her for years, then in the end had married her, defying his eminent father-in-law.

McClure had learned the publishing business in Boston at a bicycle magazine and had worked briefly in New York at the *Century,* perhaps the nation's most distinguished periodical. With his dearest friend, John S. Phillips (typically, having to convince him), he had started the McClure Syndicate. Phillips, who had been his classmate at Knox College, literary editor of their student magazine, and the best man at his wedding, would be at

Sam McClure.

John S. Phillips.

Sam's right hand for years to come. They'd signed up original works by Robert Louis Stevenson, Mark Twain, Joseph Conrad, H. G. Wells, Rudyard Kipling, Henry James, Arthur Conan Doyle, and Stephen Crane, paying one hundred or two hundred dollars to each author, then sold the stories to newspapers for five dollars each. Previously, U.S. syndicates had provided only boilerplate, or generic space fillers, to local newspapers. But Sam had an eye for excellence, ambition to bring great literature to ordinary Americans, and willingness to gamble. It seemed there was nothing he couldn't do by sheer force of personality.

He had read her piece on the paving of Parisian streets and "said to his partner, Phillips, 'This girl can write. We need to get her to do some work for our magazine.'" Yes, a new magazine! Phillips was going to be its managing editor. *McClure's Magazine* would be the most important and best-looking magazine in the world! They would outdo *Scribner's* and the *Century* and *Harper's* with the kinds of stories people were hungry for. He wanted clear, lively writing to explain the latest scientific advances, all new ideas, the wisdom and lives of great men. Ida, he had discovered, did just what he was looking for: she adapted the methods of French historical writing, clarifying complicated events and issues for a popular audience.

He listened in turn to Ida's story.

After more than three hours had elapsed, he sprang up, saying he had to catch a train to Geneva. Now the banks would be closed. Could she lend him forty dollars? Ida had exactly that amount tucked away in a drawer, saved for her vacation. She hurried to get it. He took it away, saying he found it odd that she had so much money in the house. She told him it had never happened before. He went out the door, muttering that he must have left his hat and umbrella at the Associated Press.

Ida's sensible self at once assailed her. "Fool! He's a fascinating will-of-the-wisp. I'll never see that money!" She would never dare to ask for it. So much for the vacation. But the money was wired the very next day by McClure's London office.

Ida wrote guardedly to her family. She had liked him, but he was a "hustler," "enthusiasm all through." He had said he wished she'd go back to help him in New York. What a "good joke" it would be on "the Mogul [Flood] wouldn't it? To go back into an editorial position as good as the one *McClure's* will have in a year after my scalping. But I shall not do it. I'm going to make this literary business go if there is anything for me in it."

After some time had passed, she reported to her family, "My work for *McClure's* is still rather mythical as I've not heard from him since he reached New York." Her roommates, her friend Charles Downer Hazen, and the others had all gone home. She had begun to long for home too, admitting that "I am beginning to see how it goes without intimate friends." Despite her precarious situation, she wouldn't allow herself to be dazzled by McClure. He was a great persuader and she liked him enormously. While hoping things might work out, she was prepared for them not to.

CHAPTER EIGHT

Edging Toward Home

IN ADDITION TO her writing, social outings, classes, and research for the Roland biography, Ida prepared five talks, which she delivered to gatherings of interested parties in private homes. The first of her subjects was Madame de Staël, a constitutional republican, opponent of Napoleon, novelist, and mistress of a famous salon, which conferred on her a reputation that had lasted far longer than Madame Roland's. Salons, a French institution since the late seventeenth century, were social gatherings usually hosted by a formidable woman and dedicated to witty discussion of current ideas. They were potent political as well as cultural forces. In general, French women did not demand concessions from men; they simply exploited their own gifts in institutions designed to show them off, notably the salons. French women were also mutually supportive, writers and scholars helping one another to do their best work.

In the fall of 1892, the Reverend Flood tried to make amends, long distance. He asked Ida to write two articles on the Paris salons. He would pay her one hundred dollars for them. The Tarbell family, to whom Ida reported the offer, argued against having anything to do with him. It seemed that Flood had recently insulted them again. Without specifying the slight, Ida replied to a now lost letter, "The miserable liar to talk so about Will!" She vowed not to write for Flood. But in the end she accepted the assignment and Flood's money. She thought American women needed to form mutually supportive social networks and would benefit from knowing about salons.

In the summer of 1893, *McClure's* sent August Jaccaci, the magazine's art director, to see Ida. Much of the new magazine's appeal would be in its layout and copious illustrations, so he was a key figure on the staff. Jaccaci was urbane, thoroughly likable, very well connected, and utterly at home in Paris. Ida was impressed when he took her to dinner, paid the bill, and sent her back home alone on a bus as if she were a man, instead of escorting her to her door. In August, Jaccaci cabled her from London, summoning her to a rendezvous at a café across from the Saint-Lazare train station at five thirty the next morning. She obliged, despite the ungodly hour. He had brought the maiden issue of *McClure's* to show her. She was captivated by its youthful spirit, and what she called its "lift."

Meanwhile, she enjoyed social and professional encounters with a variety of other men. The editor of *Scribner's* came to town. Ida asked him to consider publishing her work on Madame Roland. His response was encouraging, and he suggested she write articles for his magazine in the meantime. Soon afterward, Ida's old friend Laura Seaver sent a Standard Oil representative to meet her. Much to her amusement, he showed up in her tiny, inelegant room (for she no longer had a parlor) in full formal dress. They got on famously, she reported. He took her to dinner, returned her to her room, and went back to his wife. On another night, a handsome Swiss took her out. A few days later, the Standard Oil man, sick in bed, sent for her. It's hard to imagine how that scene was played; the unchaperoned visit would not have been considered respectable back home.

One day, a man leaped into the railway carriage in which Ida was sitting and kissed her. It was a case of mistaken identity. At the Bibliothèque nationale, another man tried to pick her up. Ida relished these adventures, which entertained her family and couldn't possibly have happened in Titusville. Ida also reported that she felt treated as a specimen by French people, who remarked on her intelligence as if it were cause for astonishment.

McClure's now began hiring her regularly on a freelance basis. One assignment was to interview several literary women of Paris. Ida was thrilled to find that the women not only were producing serious journalism and literature; they also lent support to one another. Her first subject enthusiastically put her in touch with writer friends. One was an advocate, in her own work, for the poor and was famous for having interviewed the pope. She remarked to Ida, "Jealousy of a woman's success is, after gallantry, the most difficult thing a French woman trying to support herself has to bear from the men she meets." To Ida's surprise, she also voiced a stirring rejection of suffrage, doubting the "usefulness" of the vote and proudly proclaiming the "self-denying and maternal role" nature had given her.

McClure dispatched Ida to the home of famed scientist Louis Pasteur, who in old age regretted that he'd been diverted from his true passion — crystals — by the study of fermentation and its application to the sanitary processing, or pasteurization, of milk, beer, and wine. She and the elderly scientist combed through his family photographs for images to serve as the illustrations that were the hallmark of any *McClure's* portrait. Ida admired Pasteur's equanimity. "This is a great man . . . so great that he despises notoriety and a journalist," she observed. "Notoriety" and its cost were suddenly becoming a matter of relevance. Publicity in the press was creating instant celebrities, people famous for being famous, overshadowing those whose recognition was earned by merit or accomplishment.

Ida returned again to the subject of women in journalism, drawing on her far more extensive experience, including the wisdom she'd gleaned from French colleagues. "A Paris Press Woman" appeared in the *Boston Transcript* on December 16, 1893. It was Ida's personal statement of purpose. Women journalists succeeded, she wrote, wherever "pluck, prompt action and racy writing" were called for, but they didn't show sustained mastery of their subjects. Women had the capacity to be more scholarly if they undertook "sincere study with constant writing." As she had said in the *Chautauquan,* fine work took "a ripened mind and long practice." Now she knew that more was required if women were to rise to the first rank. The woman writer must be able to grasp salient facts and to present them clearly and entertainingly in a context of helpful comparisons and opinions. Ida hoped she was providing a model for American women journalists who wished to do serious and lasting work. "It is not an easy model which I offer, I admit. But it is worth following." She believed that her profession was an ideal one for women.

McClure sent her back to Louis Pasteur to find out what the venerable scientist thought lay in store for the world. Her report would be part of a regular feature to be called "The Edge of the Future." Ida was excited. "It meant something more than I had dreamed possible in magazine journalism." She went on similar assignments to Emile Zola, Alphonse Daudet, and Alexandre Dumas *fils,* all eminent writers and cultural fixtures of the day.

For weeks in 1894, Ida awaited payment for her articles. Founded during the Panic of '93, one of America's worst economic downturns, *McClure's* was chronically short of funds. Ida asked her family if she could borrow fifty dollars to "pay a pressing stationery bill." She also requested a few U.S. postage stamps, which could be resold in Paris. In the end, Ida pawned her sealskin coat, producing her Allegheny diploma as identification. She was tutoring a young man in English to pay for her own French lessons and claimed that "my little baron is the saving clause of my existence." Then she sold another article to the *New England Magazine* and bought herself a few more weeks in France.

The biography of Madame Roland that she had come to Paris to write was always in the back of her mind. A wave of anarchist bombings and student riots in the city in 1893 had again spurred her thinking about the French Revolution. "Of course you have read how the dynamite has been blowing things right and left and the anarchists declaring that all Paris on May 1 was going to be bounced," she breezily reported to her family. She never did witness a bombing in progress but hoped she would, feeling it was her journalistic duty. Months later, when students rioted, she was caught in crossfire in the street and had to cower in a church vestibule.

The Bibliothèque nationale had recently acquired Madame Roland's papers, including unpublished letters to her husband, and Ida was the first researcher to examine them. French friends put her in touch with several of Roland's descendants, who invited her to stay at their country home. There she heard stories passed down in the family of the revolutionary heroine. She admired the domestic skills of the current mistress of the estate and delighted in the roses that dated from the time of the Revolution, gaily poking some blossoms into her hair.

When Ida returned to Paris from the Roland estate in the country, two solid years of research behind her, she realized that her earlier admiration for Madame Roland had been all but erased. While her biography is one of Ida's minor works, it marked a momentous turning point in her thinking about women and politics. As she put it later, "I had undertaken the study of this woman in order to clear up my mind about the quality of service that women could give and had given in public life, particularly in times of stress." She had hoped to find that Madame Roland had been a force for moderation — that, with a woman's intuition, she had worked for unselfish compromise among the factions fighting for supremacy after the French king was deposed.

Ida concluded, however, that Madame Roland had not formed independent beliefs, but rather followed her husband's lead in pushing for first a constitution and then a republic. "The reasonable girl who had welcomed Louis XVI to the throne . . . had suddenly become inexorable in her demands." Along with her husband, Madame Roland had helped to foment the violence that led to the Terror and to her own execution. "This woman had been one of the steadiest influences to violence, willing, even eager, to use this terrible revolutionary force, so bewildering and terrifying to me, to accomplish her ends, childishly believing herself and her friends strong enough to control it when they needed it no longer. The heaviest blow to my self-confidence so far was my loss of faith in revolution as a divine weapon. Not since I discovered the world not to have been made in six days . . . had I been so intellectually and spiritually upset." This volcanic reordering of her thinking left her firmly on the side of compromise and evolutionary change.

Roland had also reinforced Ida's concern about the irrationality of a woman in love. Of her, Ida wrote, "It was the woman's nature, which, stirred to its depths by enthusiasm or passion, becomes narrow, stern, unbending — which can do but one thing, can see one way; that inexplicable familiar conviction which is superior to experience, and indifferent to logic." Ida seems to have prided herself on not being susceptible to passion. It is surely what she was arming herself against when she prayed to be spared from marriage.

Ida wondered whether an American suffragist would be swayed by her finding that Roland had only backed up her man, and decided that it wasn't her concern. She had determined what women ought not to do, but so far had not found what women in a changing society could and should do.

She eventually revised her criticism of Roland, calling herself a "reactionist" who had first idealized her heroine only to find that she was a woman just like any other. Of course, Roland was not at all ordinary, but an exceptional human being who left her mark on history. Ida credited the ordinary woman with "intuitions . . . born of centuries of intimate first-hand dealing with human beings from babyhood on," which meant she would be "no party to violence." But she turned her back on her erstwhile heroine, Roland.

McClure was still urging Ida to join his staff in New York, but she continued to demur. When the magazine's Paris representative, Edward Stanton, was hired away by the Associated Press, Ida agreed to replace him. The job meant more writing and more travel. McClure was beginning to count heavily on Ida's abilities and resiliency, and probably on her abiding humility. She could make complicated technical subjects clear and dramatic; she was not one to make demands or refuse a tough assignment.

McClure offered Ida the position of youth editor at the magazine, replacing the departing Frances Hodgson Burnett. She continued to put him off, unwilling to commit to what seemed an uncertain proposition. The magazine's finances, like her own, were precarious. Sent to Britain to interview a Scottish cleric who reconciled evolution with God, she was promised an expense account but found it was ridiculously small, barely enough for oatmeal porridge for dinner. "As usual, I'm on the ragged edge of bankruptcy and gay as a cricket about it. The McClures are very taken with my work, so they write me," she told her family. Sam had demanded to know if she planned to get married—he intended to invest in her over the long term. She was longing to go home so she could regroup and finish her book. "If McClure wants me and has the money he can have me," she declared, "but it must be for money this time."

Sam knew what he wanted: this relatively unknown provincial woman writer who'd never even spent time in New York. He poured on the persuasion. He took Ida to lunch in London. She ordered the most expensive dishes while he praised the accuracy of her writing, a superfluous compliment she afterward compared to being told she could add.

Ida, age thirty-six, in the dress she repeatedly altered to wear on different occasions.

He offered to pay for some new clothes (Ida had been repeatedly altering the same dress for different occasions) and for her passage home; he granted her several months' leave in Titusville to reunite with her family and offered her a starting annual salary of $2,100, which would soon rise to $3,000. He promised her she'd be rich in fifteen years. But Ida's instincts were correct. Sam had only the $150 to cover her fare home. At the time, he did not even know if his magazine was still being published.

Ida knew *McClure's* was practically bankrupt; even so, Sam did have the money to get her home. Besides, he was irresistibly charismatic. His college landlady had gushed, "He could hardly pass my door but that I felt the influence of his vitality." Ida was susceptible too. She gave in and boarded a ship with the intention, after she'd had a long rest, of returning to Paris and writing for *Scribner's* as well as *McClure's*. She pictured herself living in a charming garret among the rooftops of the Latin Quarter in the future, hosting her own salon, "while [she] cleared up [her] mind on women and revolution and continued [her] search for God in the great cathedrals." Her heart still belonged to Paris.

CHAPTER NINE

McClure's

*I*T'S HARD TO say whether Sam McClure revolutionized American journalism or simply exploited a rising opportunity. The newspaper syndicate he'd founded in the 1880s was the first company of its kind to earn a profit. His charm and enthusiasm persuaded most of the great authors of the day to write for *McClure's,* and it was in its pages that many Americans read these writers' work for the first time.

Sam had invented the general-interest Sunday newspaper supplement, filling it with book reviews, recipes, and serials. He built a huge new reading audience and then fed it material he bought in Europe, making eight round trips between 1887 and 1893. ("Where is my wandering boy tonight?" asked his wife.) All the while, he dreamed of a magazine and decided that 1893 was the perfect time to start one.

Before the stock market crashed that year, sales of consumer goods had doubled, matching the growth of a population with more money and more leisure time than ever before. A magazine would be the best advertising medium for the new businesses operating nationwide.

The technology of photographic reproduction had improved, making better-quality illustrations possible. High-speed printing presses made publishing cheaper. Postage rates had fallen, and postal delivery reached the most remote homesteads. Public schools had multiplied and literacy rates were up.

Only the economic crisis, increasing signs of which, in his hyperactive preparations, Sam hadn't paid attention to, complicated his efforts. The company was strapped, and writers, including Ida, weren't paid. But Sam plunged ahead. John Phillips put up the $7,300 that launched *McClure's*.

Sam's greatest enthusiasm was for breakthroughs in science, the ideas of the future. But he'd found that scientists couldn't write. When Ida's article on Paris street paving landed on his desk in 1893, he loved it. Who was she? Phillips replied, "From the looks of her handwriting, she's a middle aged New England schoolmarm."

"She can write!" said Sam. Ida remarked later that Phillips "knew the value of naturalness, detested fake style."

What she called "fake style" was the literary pretentiousness of the "best" magazines of the nineteenth century. They were geared toward the genteel eastern upper-middle-class reader who could afford to pay thirty-five cents an issue. Sam considered himself a midwesterner, as was Phillips, whose family lived in Galesburg, Illinois. They felt they understood the aspirations of people in the vast American heartland. To reach this audience, Sam decided that *McClure's* would sell for about half of what its rivals charged. The price of a copy eventually dropped from fifteen to only ten cents.

Sam opened his first office at 743 Broadway in New York City in 1893. He was offered the chance to publish Stephen Crane's Civil War novel *The Red Badge of Courage* but lacked funds to buy it, having blown the last of his cash on returning Ida to Titusville.

Undaunted, Sam established what would be his pattern. He kept the office in a constant state of upheaval and underwent periods of nervous exhaustion that were relieved only by Atlantic crossings. In London or Paris some new idea would come along to revive him. He sent his staff a stream of press clippings, all of them potential stories. To lose enthusiasm was the worst thing that could happen to an editor, he said.

Back in New York, he barked, "What are you doing? No matter what it is, put it away and go home. Lay on my desk tomorrow a list of twenty ideas, twenty good ones. Now get on!" Twenty thousand copies of the first issue, the one Jaccaci showed to Ida at dawn in Paris, were printed, and twelve thousand were returned unsold. But most of those who read it were impressed. A critic declared it fresh and challenging. "It throbs with actuality from beginning to end." That immediacy had to be reintroduced every time.

The great Kansas newspaper editor William Allen White wrote for *McClure's*. He said that Sam had hunches, but John Phillips, the managing editor, "blew on the spark of genius." Phillips, tall, soft-spoken, steady as a rock, with "honesty of heart and soul," was "the power belt that carried the force of Sam's engine to make the enterprise go."

The *Century,* the principal rival of *McClure's,* announced a series of articles about Napoleon Bonaparte, who had made himself emperor of France after the Revolution. France had recently celebrated his centennial. A reader in Omaha suggested to Sam that *McClure's* commission its own series. Sam was already running a feature called "Human Documents," chronicling in pictures the lives of celebrities from infancy to old age. When he learned of a massive collection of Napoleon images owned by attorney and philanthropist Gardiner Hubbard, he commissioned the poet Wordsworth's grandson to write a biography to accompany them. The first installment was scheduled for November 1894. Wordsworth's grandson, however, did not disguise his contempt for Bonaparte. Concerned that his collection of images would be ill served by a disrespectful text, Hubbard vetoed it in August.

What to do? Sam instantly resolved to telegraph Ida, who was enjoying a reunion with her family in Titusville, to come at once and take on the assignment. Had she stayed in Paris, where the primary materials lay, she reflected, rather than accepting his invitation to go home, she might have written a far more comprehensive biography. But now she was in the United States and would have to make do with available material. It would take some digging. Unlike other editors, who paid only for finished articles, Sam would support her while she researched. At *McClure's,* writers were not to churn articles out, but to become "experts" on their subjects.

Bonapartists in Paris were hoping to restart the dynasty, so French readers would be interested in the series. But why on earth, Ida wondered, would a popular American magazine undertake a biography of a long-dead Frenchman? On the other hand, Napoleon had modernized France after the Revolution. Understanding how he had done it would help round out her study of Madame Roland. Furthermore, Sam offered to pay her the unheard-of sum of forty dollars a week. "It was laughable. And yet how could I refuse to try?" she wrote later.

After a brief sojourn in New York, Ida set off—not for Paris, but for the Hubbards' country home in Chevy Chase,

Gardiner Hubbard with his wife, Gertrude.

Maryland, where the images of Napoleon were stored. Hubbard insisted that she base herself there so that he could keep tabs on her work. Further research was to be conducted at the Library of Congress in Washington, D.C.

Ida felt out of place in the Hubbards' home — too plain, not dressed elegantly enough, still shy. Sam disconcerted her by repeatedly popping in without warning, creating a ruckus, flinging proofs of articles all over the carpets. Raised to be ladylike, Ida felt she must apologize for his behavior, but Mrs. Hubbard brushed it off, saying, "That eagerness of his is beautiful. I am accustomed to geniuses."

Ida was delighted to find friends from Chautauqua and Paris at Johns Hopkins University in nearby Baltimore. John Martin Vincent, a historian of medieval Switzerland, and his wife, Ada, a painter, introduced their handsome bachelor friend Professor Herbert B. Adams to Ida, and the four shared many outings. A historian, Adams emphasized objective interpretation of primary sources — something that was becoming Ida's method as well. Perhaps they discussed the role of women through history, for she later displayed a detailed knowledge of the subject. Adams was a

Herbert B. Adams.

proponent of women's education and taught at both Hopkins and the all-female Smith College. Ida consulted him while she did her research and he sent her books that he thought would interest her.

Sam was determined to publish the Napoleon series while the *Century*'s version was still running, and to outsell it. Working even more feverishly

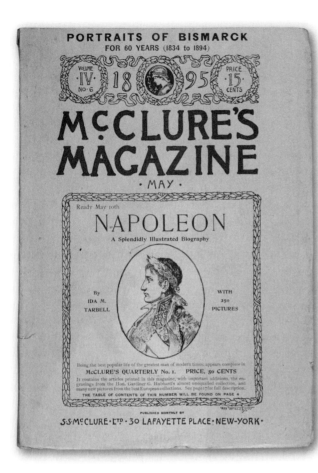

The cover of McClure's with an installment of the Napoleon series.

than usual, Ida produced a first installment in six weeks. Napoleon, she concluded, was "the greatest genius of his time, perhaps of all time; yet he lacked the crown of greatness — that high wisdom born of reflection and introspection which knows its own powers and limitations and never abuses them; that fine sense of proportion which holds the rights of others in the same solemn reverence it demands for its own." Unlike the efforts of the French Revolutionaries, which in her view had been destructive, Napoleon's civic reforms were constructive.

Ida referred to her biography as a "tongue in cheek . . . sketch" but it more than fulfilled the hopes of Mr. Hubbard. Critics, experts, and a Bonaparte descendant all endorsed it. To Sam's delight, the circulation of *McClure's* doubled while the series ran in seven long installments (a total of 156 pages of text), each lavishly illustrated, from November 1894 to April 1895. "Napoleon" became a best-selling book and earned royalties for Ida for the rest of her life. She continued to receive letters from readers for many years, including one offering to sell her a chair that had belonged to Napoleon himself. Sam made certain Ida knew that *McClure's* was her new permanent home.

Scribner's, too, was impressed by the success of "Napoleon" and finally agreed to publish Ida's biography of Madame Roland. Young writers were clearly awed when introduced to Ida in person, and although she seemed outwardly indifferent to fame, her circumstances were permanently altered. Suddenly, her writing career was no longer a matter of chance and struggle. She acknowledged the change with her usual modesty: "[The] sketch [of Napoleon shaped] my outward life in spite of me . . . [and] turned my plans topsy-turvy."

Back in the New York office of *McClure's*, Ida was hailed as the asset she

Sam McClure (left) and John Phillips shared an office at the magazine.

had shown herself to be. She, in turn, took easily to the collegial atmosphere, which could veer from elation to alarm. Sam, known as the General, was "as eager as a dog on the hunt," Ida thought. His office visits were erratic, but when he was present, he stirred excitement, kept everyone on edge, insisted on perfection. In addition to new work by Rudyard Kipling, Arthur Conan Doyle, Thomas Hardy, and Mark Twain, he had managed to sign up the first articles about the x-ray, Marconi's wireless radio, and the Wright brothers' airplane. At the same time, Sam was susceptible to down-and-outers, offering employment to "a string of derelicts ranging from aristocratic scrub ladies to indigent editors," leaving it to Phillips to find work for them.

Ida credited Phillips's "nose for humbug" and "patience when dealing with the impatient" with usually saving the day. Tall, dignified, unflappable, owlish Phillips was the most intellectual and best educated member of the staff. Until they were both in late middle age, Ida called him Mr. Phillips, managing to imbue the formal title with affection.

But Ida was not to stay put in New York quite yet. Sam had another idea for her.

Abraham Lincoln had been dead less than thirty years. As with Napoleon, there was a wave of renewed popular interest in Lincoln, and rival magazines were churning out articles about him. The rest of the *McClure's* staff felt it would be a mistake to copy another feature, but Sam's interest in Lincoln was an obsession that had been fostered in Galesburg, in the heart of Lincoln country. He was sure some fresh proof of Lincoln's greatness lay out in the field to be discovered. To Ida he said, "Out with you. Look. See. Report." She would follow Lincoln's path from Kentucky to Indiana to Illinois to Washington, ferreting out anecdotes and images—daguerreotypes never before seen, if possible! To unearth new material, she was to interview everyone still living who had known Lincoln personally before he became president.

The *Century* had just serialized a biography by Lincoln's private secretaries, John Nicolay and John Hay, who had access to a wealth of private papers. Asked what he thought of the *McClure's* assignment, the *Century's* editor sneered, "They got a girl to write a Life of Lincoln."

In Washington, Ida consulted Nicolay, who was offended by her incursion into his territory and refused to cooperate. He asserted that hers was a hopeless assignment, as he and Hay had told all that was worth telling of Lincoln's life. Nicolay's rebuff forced Ida to approach Lincoln through his origins: "I would not begin at the end of the story with the great and known but at the start in Kentucky with the humble and unknown." Among its other advantages, beginning at the beginning would keep her from becoming bored with her subject as she built his life story.

A Washington acquaintance introduced her to Lincoln's eldest son, Robert Lincoln, who said he had only one early unpublished daguerreotype to give her. The public was accustomed to portraits of a worn older Lincoln that suggested he was depressed. The daguerreotype proved to be myth shattering: it showed that Lincoln had been no homely, disheveled rube and didn't even look particularly sad. The new image made the perfect striking frontispiece for the series.

But this was to be living history as well. Ida set forth on her odyssey, seeking out those who could tell her what Lincoln was like. A lone woman on the road, sleeping in rough country hotels, asking questions and taking photographs, put the locals on their guard. Ida carefully won people's trust, charmed them out of their mementoes, and showed such kindness to her sources — trying to solve problems they confided — that many wrote gratefully to her afterward with updates on their circumstances. She was amused to find of Lincoln's acquaintances that "few of them even to this day understand how one of them could have become President. From them seems to be hidden a proper appreciation of his gifts."

People kept mentioning a lost speech delivered by Lincoln in 1856. Everyone remembered how great it was, but no one had written it down. Ida's news nose told her that couldn't be true. She searched and searched for someone who had made notes. She was repeatedly told to give up, but would not. She finally found Henry Clay Whitney in Massachusetts. He had taken notes and kept them. Ida took them to several other witnesses to the speech and asked if the notes seemed accurate to them. The deciding vote for their authenticity came from the editor of the *Chicago Tribune*. But, as Ida wryly noted, she wasn't able to convince a few die-hards who were wedded to the idea that the Lost Speech was lost forever. Whitney published a version of the speech, based on his notes, in *McClure's* in 1896. Historians have since dismissed Whitney's account of the speech, which is presumed to have been a vigorous denunciation of slavery and therefore perhaps deliberately "lost."

Ida visited Knox College, Sam McClure's alma mater and site of the fifth campaign debate between Lincoln and Senator Stephen Douglas in 1858. At Knox, with the help of John H. Finley, the nation's youngest college president, she found "the stirring and picturesque material that I sought." Finley had been a student of her friend Herbert B. Adams at Johns Hopkins and had known Ida at the *Chautauquan*. He would later contribute to Ida's work on Standard Oil and become editor of the *New York Times*.

All over the country, people harbored Lincoln memories and memorabilia. Finding them meant writing letters to hundreds, awaiting their replies, sifting leads, following them, evaluating them. Letters went astray; people who might have information fell ill or died. When someone produced Lincoln correspondence or an anecdote, Ida had to confirm its source and authenticity. Tracking down the images also required the dispatch of letters by the hundreds.

Dashing back and forth from New York or Washington to interview people in the field, Ida found more than three hundred previously unpublished Lincoln speeches and letters, pictures never seen by the public, and many personal anecdotes. An initial request to review a collection of Civil War records was denied on the grounds that a woman couldn't possibly understand them. But she prevailed in the end.

Ida was drawn into a few wild-goose chases. After intensive sleuthing that took her all the way to Europe, where her old friends rejoiced in her success, a rumor that Lincoln had written Queen Victoria to beg her not to recognize the Confederacy was shown to be false. Her companion on that trip was her sister, Sarah, seeing foreign lands for the first time. Sarah decided to stay behind in Paris to paint.

In her determination to scrub the Lincoln family's reputation, Ida claimed that Nancy Hanks, Lincoln's mother, was not illegitimate. Years later, Ida had to admit that she was wrong. She avoided idealizing or romanticizing Lincoln, but she did repeat unproven stories that appealed to her, such as one about a tragic premarital romance.

Drawing on her own childhood to understand Lincoln's, Ida portrayed a man whom only pioneer America could have produced and whose native greatness saved the nation. She attributed his rise to early ambition and hard study. The biography reaffirmed "the values of the old America at a time when they were seemingly ineffective in countering the changes sweeping

Ida around 1898.

over the nation." She dedicated the book to her father, who was endowed, she felt, with Lincolnesque virtues that derived from the frontier experience and had enriched the American character: keen intellect, wit, inventiveness and practical skills, courage, humor, and honesty.

When each article was completed, the proofs were sent out to those whose information had been included so that they might double-check them for accuracy. This process could take weeks, but it was the only method available. Ida didn't use a typewriter; she dictated many letters and handwrote more. The letters she received were nearly all written by hand, in ink and even in pencil, in a bewildering variety of hard-to-decipher scrawls.

Sam's practice was to read every installment three times. If by then his interest had flagged, Ida rewrote that piece. He insisted that people and actions be characterized by examples rather than adjectives and that incidents be allowed to speak for themselves, without editorialization. Ida easily complied with this order, unlike certain emotional reporters, who had often to be reminded that it was documentation, not high-flown rhetoric, that would make an article influential. They protested that facts could be just as false as opinions.

Sam had been correct about the public's appetite for a new telling of

Lincoln's life. The twelve-part series of 1895–96 raised the circulation of *McClure's* to over 300,000, higher than any rival magazine's. The name Ida M. Tarbell became known to ordinary Americans everywhere. Late in life, Ida remarked that Lincoln had never bored her and that working on his biography had made her decide to become a writer rather than an editor. Her trove of anecdotes and reminiscences was deployed in magazine articles for Lincoln's birthday for decades to come, and most were eventually collected in books. Ida had helped to make Lincoln an exemplar of egalitarian American ideals. A man once "jeered," as she said, was now "the simple, steady, resolute, unselfish man whose supreme ambition was to find out the truth."

The magazine's paid advertising increased so much during the Lincoln

A newsstand near the McClure's office displays the wealth of periodicals available to readers.

series that Sam decided to buy a printing plant and a bindery. He borrowed to do it; like Rockefeller, he never hesitated to go into debt, but he wasn't as careful about paying back the money. The modern press improved the reproduction of illustrations, so important to *McClure's*. The magazine moved to the top floor of a building that covered an entire acre on Lexington Avenue between Twenty-Fifth and Twenty-Sixth Streets. Sam added Stephen Crane to his roster of writers, eliciting some of his best short stories and a harsh description of coal mining. Future classics, such as Joseph Conrad's *Heart of Darkness,* Bram Stoker's *Dracula,* and stories by Jack London and Robert Louis Stevenson, were all eagerly read in *McClure's.*

Sam brought Frank Doubleday on board as vice president of *McClure's* and president of a separate book company, Doubleday & McClure, which published Ida's Lincoln book. But when Sam pressured the book publisher to become a *McClure's* subsidiary, Doubleday quit, taking *McClure's* editor Walter Hines Page with him and forming a new company. He also lured Rudyard Kipling away. Sam's genius as an editor was matched by neither financial discipline nor psychological insight. Ida and several colleagues were dismayed by the episode.

Ignoring staff tension, Sam demanded that they create stories of the now, of its effect on the future. Ideas for articles came to him in a white heat. One colleague said Sam had an idea a minute and only John Phillips knew which one wasn't crazy. What about inventor Nikola Tesla, immigration, the income tax proposal, the

Carl Schurz.

increase in crime, the horseless carriage, wild animals, consolidation in big business? Then he bolted for the Middle East to see for himself the setting for a life of Jesus — with what else could they follow Napoleon and Lincoln? Journalist Lincoln Steffens called him "the wild editor."

Ida was looking for her next big story. She had interviewed Carl Schurz about his memories of Lincoln. A German immigrant who became a great American patriot, Schurz had served as a reformer in Congress and as secretary of the interior. Ida thought his reminiscences would make a grand feature for the magazine, and he agreed. She loved working with him and did so for several years. He was amusing, frank, and unpredictable. She may have been a little in love with him.

Researching the Lincoln articles had taken her back to Washington and the accomplished social circle of the Hubbards and Alexander Graham Bells. Lanky Ida, who once thought herself too dowdy, discussed the latest developments in science and affairs of state with powerful men and their wives over dinner. She had established herself as an independent-minded woman of substance and accomplishment, living on her own in the world. It didn't go to her head; increased readership only meant increased scrutiny and the continuing challenge to produce superior work.

CHAPTER TEN

An Imperial Nation

REPUBLICAN WILLIAM MCKINLEY'S defeat of Democrat William Jennings Bryan in the 1896 presidential election was financed for the first time by unlimited campaign contributions from moneyed interests. It ended the populist movement's turn on the national stage. The Republican Party, which had once stood for the abolition of slavery, was now the eager servant of big business. The strikes of the 1880s and their violent suppression by hired guns allied with police and members of the National Guard had left workers embittered and helpless. Farming was becoming mechanized, forcing farmers into debt to buy equipment and land. Many were unable to borrow and lost their property.

In 1897, Theodore Roosevelt, who was then the assistant secretary of the navy, wrote to a friend, "In strict confidence, I would welcome almost any war, for I think this country needs one." Soon he was telling the National War College, "All great masterful races have been fighting races. . . . No triumph of peace is quite as great as the triumph of war." Roosevelt was the great champion of the strenuous life,

Colonel Theodore Roosevelt of the Rough Riders.

which found expression not only in war talk but also in ardor for fitness, sport, boys' clubs, and camping. While women began to demand a role in public life, men adorned themselves with theatrically huge mustaches and side whiskers. Masculine fitness became a kind of religion. Muscles swelled and battleships acquired bigger guns.

American exports were lagging. Now that western territorial expansion was complete, surplus goods were piling up and overseas markets were needed to absorb them. Those markets could be acquired in a war. Roosevelt and others believed that war would also shape up the nation and serve to channel the unrest that had built up among the lower classes.

Ida was conducting interviews with Nelson A. Miles, commanding general of the U.S. Army, for a series meant to feed the public's growing interest in military affairs. She and Sam attributed this interest to fear of revolution, as well as to strained relations with Spain.

One of Spain's colonies was a close neighbor of North America — Cuba. Cubans were rioting for their independence. The battleship *Maine* was dispatched to Havana Harbor to protect American interests. In February 1898, just when Ida was scheduled to meet with General Miles, someone blew up the *Maine*. He didn't cancel their appointment, so Ida was at army headquarters and witnessed the response to the explosion. Factions in the American press believed that Spain was responsible and urged U.S. intervention on Cuba's behalf.

Ida thought that everybody in the government made a good-faith effort to avoid war with Spain except Theodore Roosevelt, who kept bursting into Miles's office "like a boy on roller skates" with questions and unsolicited advice. He was already organizing the Rough Riders, a private militia with himself in charge, for an invasion. Ida was offended by the bellicose display and felt Roosevelt ought to have first resigned his civilian job in the Department of the Navy.

Senator George Frisbie Hoar of Massachusetts, who lived in the same boarding house as Ida, spoke out forcefully against colonizing undeveloped nations such as Cuba for their natural resources, proving himself a hero of anti-imperialism. Ida's heart still belonged to France, but Hoar's opposition to war helped draw it home. "You are a part of this democratic system," she told herself. "Is it not your business to use your profession to serve it?" She realized that in France she had been merely a spectator with no duty to participate. Now her patriotism was awakened. "Between Lincoln and the Spanish-American War [as it became known] I realized I was taking on a citizenship I had practically resigned," she wrote later.

The McKinley administration and American business interests wanted Spain out of Cuba. In the end, it seemed the fastest way to accomplish that was through military force. The "splendid little war" with Spain lasted three months. Spain was driven out of Cuba. American companies moved in to claim the island's resources. The United States annexed former Spanish colonies Puerto Rico, Guam, Wake Island, and the Philippines, as well as the formerly independent Kingdom of Hawaii. The Philippines was the strategic plum, providing a base from which to compete with European and Japanese interests in China.

The Filipinos resisted an American takeover. But after three years of bloody fighting, in which 700,000 died of wounds, disease, or famine, the Philippine insurgents were crushed. Preeminent Harvard philosopher William James called U.S. conduct "one protracted infamy toward the islanders and one protracted lie towards ourselves."

A cartoon ("If They'll Only Be Good") ridiculing America's imperialistic behavior toward the conquered Philippines.

President McKinley told the nation he had prayed for guidance in dealing with the conquered peoples. He reported this revelation: "Educate, and uplift and civilize and Christianize them," and assured his constituents that after resolving to put it into effect, he "went to bed and went to sleep and slept soundly." The United States had become an imperial power overnight, with a record of atrocities committed against people of color overseas. But as Roosevelt had anticipated, the war restored prosperity.

Ida began to feel she was being pulled off course. As her passion for France ebbed and she gave up the dream of leading a salon on the Left Bank, she was afraid she'd lose touch with her friends in Paris. But America's economic and social problems dwarfed such selfish concerns. She remembered that Lincoln had intended an era of forgiveness and healing to follow the Civil War, "with malice toward none" as he had declared in his second inaugural address. Instead, the Jim Crow era of segregation and brutality was in many ways worse for blacks than slavery had been. Industrial workers, too, seemed consigned to an insidious, because less obvious, form of slavery to their machines. And the post–Civil War epidemic of greed and corruption threatened democratic principles as nothing had before.

So far, Ida hadn't tackled any of these issues in her work. But there was great potential for doing so. Her income was assured by a periodical that had dedicated itself to truth telling. This was a different kind of security from the suffocating one Chautauqua had provided. "Chiefly [the appeal of *McClure's*] was the sense of vitality, of adventure, of excitement, that I was getting from being admitted on terms of equality and good comradeship into the McClure crowd," she wrote later. She had understood back in Chautauqua days that journalism offered women a unique chance to be accepted by peers — even by men — and to shine, if they worked hard and were scrupulous. And now she had earned her place in its ranks as an equal.

A Greenwich Village street fair.

In 1899, Sam summoned Ida from Washington, where she had been based while writing the Napoleon and Lincoln series, to New York to be desk editor of *McClure's,* which meant she would run the office. She rented an apartment on a tree-lined street off Fifth Avenue in Greenwich Village because the area reminded her of Paris. The Village, with its irregular streets and low gracious houses, hadn't yet reached its peak as a hotbed of bohemian artists, intellectuals, and radicals, but many of them had already settled there.

The windows in Ida's parlor, overlooking the street, stretched nearly to the floor and filled the room with light. She used one of the two bedrooms as her study. A pair of cats kept her company, and an Irish maid did the housekeeping. In the evening, she often dined at the Hotel Brevoort on Fifth Avenue or at a cozy French restaurant on a side street, both frequented by Mark Twain. Ida was bohemian in that she maintained her Paris customs;

a woman dining alone, or even with another woman as aristocratic as Ida's frequent companion, Mrs. Schuyler Van Rensselaer, flouted the usual rules of respectability in New York.

The wealthy, widowed Mrs. Van Rensselaer was America's first female architecture critic, writing for the *Century* and publishing several books. Reflecting long afterward on their friendship, Ida said, "I was deeply attached to her; she belonged to such a different world but there was always a bridge over [the divide] and we came and went naturally on it."

The friends had more than their careers in common. Van Rensselaer had published a pamphlet in 1894 strongly opposing women's suffrage, arguing that to have the vote and thus to be drawn into political activities would lead mothers to neglect their families. At the turn of the century, running a household consumed far more time and energy than we can appreciate, now that labor-saving technology has made some housekeeping tasks of the nineteenth century obsolete. Household and family management was equivalent to a career. Anti-suffragists also warned that women should be shielded from the coarseness of politics, and Ida agreed.

Sam appointed Ida desk editor because he planned to be away from the office for several months and needed someone in place who had a cool head and an apparently inexhaustible capacity for hard work. None of her predecessors had held the job for very long. Someone once suggested throwing a party for all the men and women who had been desk editors at *McClure's* and was told it wasn't practical — they'd "have to rent Madison Square Garden." In accepting the post, Ida was rewarded with shares in the company and the highest salary the industry offered: $5,000 a year. Sam was the magazine's proprietor, and now Ida, along with Phillips, was also part owner.

Photographs of Ida in her office show her sitting a bit self-consciously at her desk, dressed for work in shirtwaist and tie and a stiff, ankle-length skirt

Ida poses in her office attire at McClure's, 1898.

in the mode of Charles Dana Gibson's popular illustrations, her long, dark, abundant hair piled in a bun. The "Gibson girl" was the spirited feminine icon of the 1890s, a newly independent female who played golf and tennis and could wrap a man around her little finger — at least until she married him, when her scant measure of independence was gone.

Ida quickly became the imperturbable anchor of the *McClure's* office, with John Phillips making the day-to-day decisions. When Sam wasn't out taking the pulse of the nation or signing up a famous author, he ricocheted around the place, complaining that the magazine was stale, needed fresh ideas, more juice. For one staffer, "McClure was the motor, Phillips and Ida were the control. I can see her still, sitting there and gravely weighing prospects, possibilities, checking errors, soothing difference." Ida "held the lamp of integrity." She had total confidence in Phillips, as well as deep affection for him.

The Spanish-American War had made the magazine as sensitive to the duties of citizenship as it had Ida. Devoting an entire issue to the fighting, Sam had sent Stephen Crane to cover Cuba. New experts on public policy were hired to report. The first to arrive was Ray Stannard Baker, who had admired Ida's Lincoln series. Only twenty-seven, he had proved himself a courageous reporter. He had covered the Pullman strike of African American railway

Ray Stannard Baker.

sleeping-car porters who were forced to live in company housing, for which they paid most of their wages. He had reported on vice in Chicago and on the army of the unemployed named for their populist leader, Coxey, in 1894. When Baker came to New York, Sam was on one of his frequent sojourns in Europe. As Baker recalled later, he was received by "Miss Tarbell, Jaccaci and Phillips. I was in the most stimulating, yes intoxicating, editorial atmosphere then existent in America — or anywhere else." In time Baker, cautious and introspective, was to earn a reputation as the nation's top journalist. A formidable group of investigative journalists was coming together at *McClure's*.

The fiction editor was Viola Roseboro', a preacher's daughter who had been an actor and a writer. An "advanced" woman who swore, smoked cigarettes she rolled herself, and dabbled in mysticism, "Rosie" tended toward intense friendships in which she played the dominant role. Ida loved Rosie's wit, colorful conversation, enthusiasms, "Spartan" courage — and probably her habitual defense of the underdog.

Professionally, Rosie had an unerring instinct for the gems among the unsolicited manuscripts that were kept

Viola Roseboro'.

in two barrels next to her desk. Screening them took no small effort; in those days, the typewriter was considered equipment for office workers, not creative people, and manuscripts were all submitted in longhand. Among her discoveries were O. Henry, Jack London, and Willa Cather. Nothing could be published without Sam's okay; when he didn't acknowledge the excellence of some manuscript she championed, Roseboro' didn't hesitate to use tears to bring him around.

In 1899 John Huston Finley resigned as president of Knox College to edit *Harper's Magazine,* which Sam, in one of his expansionist moods, had just bought. There wasn't enough money to support the debt-ridden Harper Brothers empire, so the deal unraveled very quickly. Finley joined the editorial office at *McClure's* instead.

Life at *McClure's* was both stressful and fun. Famous writers dropped by to shoot the breeze. The magazine's physical plant impressed visitors as a temple of tomorrow, with the latest linotype and photoengraving printing presses, pneumatic tubes, and an elevator big enough to hold a stagecoach and team. Lunches might last so long that it would be time to dress for dinner when they ended. New York was a small world in those days, and the *McClure's* staff knew they occupied its nerve center. Ida quickly became not just one of the boys, but, at forty-two, their esteemed coequal.

CHAPTER ELEVEN

Finding a Mission

*T*HE MAGAZINE WAS in an unsettled condition as the new century began. Sam was itching to expand, but the rash acquisition of the failing Harper Brothers enterprise was a near disaster. The magazine survived it, but the strain sent Sam reeling to Johns Hopkins Hospital and then to France. Ida had helped to arrange for *McClure's* to publish *National Geographic Magazine,* and her old favorite, *Popular Science Monthly,* was also added to the company's holdings, but that didn't amount to an empire, and Sam was imperial at heart. Although the circulation of *McClure's* hit 400,000, and its advertising revenues were better than any other magazine's, expenses were soaring too, and "the wolf was ever puffing at the door."

Sam regularly had to be revived at hospitals or spas. While today he might be diagnosed as bipolar with attention deficit disorder, in turn-of-the-century America his condition was loosely termed nervous excitement or neurasthenia. Nervousness was considered necessary to power a productive life, but too much of it led to collapse. Specialists thought people had only so much nervous energy and must conserve it. Bed rest was prescribed for women with symptoms of excitability, while men were sent out west to build themselves up. Spas for the "rest cure" abounded in the United States and abroad.

Like Sam, Ida was given to working until she was exhausted. The demands on her time seemed impossible, yet her output was immense, and she managed to squeeze in regular holidays. In addition, she was increasingly carrying the burden of holding her family together. When she reached her limit, she repaired to the handsome new sanitarium at Clifton Springs, near Rochester, New York. She happily dangled a "No Admittance" card from her doorknob and laid aside all cares for a few weeks. Charles Downer Hazen, her great friend from Paris, answered a joking letter she wrote him from Clifton Springs with his own dry humor: "So far from being amused that you are in a sanitarium I am on the contrary alarmed and indignant. Really, a Miss Tarbell sitting up only two hours a day can't be the one I know and I wish her henceforth to sit bolt erect for at least 20 a day as hitherto."

Others thought Ida's sick leave in 1899 a graver matter. A Meadville acquaintance reported that Ida's old nemesis the Reverend Flood had asked him to "look after Miss Tarbell for she is a girl of unusual intellect and *if she gets well* she will make her mark in the literary world." Another congratulated Ida on recovering from her "ordeal." Both correspondents ended by asking Ida for favors.

The staff at *McClure's* had become a kind of family. Ida took on the role of benevolent big sister. Viola Roseboro', ever the friendly rival, discounted Ida's affectionate side, maintaining that "her life largely consisted in holding people off." Nonetheless, she compared Ida favorably to another woman editor who flaunted her position and was resented by younger men on the staff. In contrast, young staffers at *McClure's* adored Ida because she wielded authority with such humility and did not resort to feminine wiles. "She seemed to the naked eye to have no coquetries at all," observed Roseboro'.

This was how Ida had always behaved with men and most women: she was simply herself, without artifice, her dry humor softening her rectitude. She did, however, generally prefer masculine company. Hazen told her, "You are the one woman I have known to whom one doesn't have to explain things. You take things like a man . . . without endless analysis." Surely discretion was part of her appeal for McClure, who felt he had to insist that she take credit for her successes. He sent her an appreciation: "I want you to realize that you have grown very precious to all of us and especially to me. I used to be so eager about business that I allowed you to be sacrificed to our work. Now I feel just the reverse. You are infinitely more important yourself to me than any work you can do. You have my heartfelt respect and love."

——— ✳ ———

In 1900 and 1901, Ida was helping Sam sift through ideas for a great feature worthy of his magazine's growing influence. She was gaining a reputation for knowing what the public craved that impressed even McClure. He said later to Lincoln Steffens, "If Miss Tarbell likes a thing, it means fifty thousand will like it. That's something to go by."

Ida and Sam shared a reverence for a bygone uncorrupted America. As an immigrant boy, Sam had believed that the U.S. government was the epitome of institutions. Civic life had been neglected during the struggle to end slavery. The Civil War represented the nation's finest hour, but it had opened "avenues for corruption. . . . The American people went on believing they were still what they once had been, but they were not." He wanted to do his part to restore the ideal.

Exposing the ills of American society would mean investing huge amounts of time and energy in travel and research. It would be expensive and dangerous, as well as an invitation to libel suits, and would require exceptionally skilled writing and editing. But McClure was always ready to go out on a limb. He had gathered the talent for the job. As desk editor, Ida could define the qualities of a new series without worrying about having to write it.

Discussions about this major project continued for months, but the editorial team couldn't make up its mind about what the focus should be. The magazine's success increased the pressure to produce something groundbreaking. More advertisers leaned on them to keep raising circulation, which meant the contents must be irresistible to a public that had ever greater choices in leisure reading.

The magazine's fiction offerings were the first to foreshadow reporting about slum life and the laboring class. *McClure's* also published an article by Ray Stannard Baker titled "The New Prosperity," a tribute to big business. After this and other flattering portraits of business and businessmen appeared in the magazine, Ida and the editors felt an increasing obligation to spotlight the huge gap between rich and poor in the United States and the corruption that fed it. Unfairness had been Ida's obsession since childhood. She was not, however, ruled by her emotions. She wanted solid reporting and balance, not partisan rant. The subject they chose must be thoroughly and objectively explained. And it had to hold readers' interest with human drama.

The Spanish-American War had, as hoped, opened new markets to American companies, along with new sources for raw materials. In 1899, hundreds of trusts — companies owning stock in other companies, called holding companies — representing billions of dollars were incorporated in New Jersey alone, where the law had recently been changed to allow them. This intermingling of businesses was organized to disguise their operations and was the arrangement central to trusts. The powerful men who created trusts found ways to smother competition, restrain trade, get cut rates for materials and services, and operate in total secrecy. They amassed kingly fortunes by forcing competitors to join them or go under. At a time when the average American worker earned ten dollars a week, Rockefeller was usually pulling in ten to twenty million a year, and there was no income tax. In one eight-month period, he earned over fifty-five million.

Starting around 1890, reformers denounced monopolies and their social cost, which included rising poverty and crime as a result of the concentration of wealth in the upper stratum of society. Reform candidates for office demanded the direct election of U.S. senators, rather than their appointment by state legislators; a progressive income tax, with the rich paying a higher percentage of their earnings than the poor; and prohibition of liquor, gambling, and prostitution. Movement toward reform led later historians to call this period the Progressive Era.

Theodore Roosevelt was picked to run for vice president with McKinley on the Republican ticket in 1900. Roosevelt had been elected governor of New York on a platform committed to reforming government and regulating industry, and once in office, he began to tax and regulate New York State's oil industry, although he accepted campaign contributions from a Standard Oil executive. He was convinced that Standard Oil had engineered his nomination for the mostly ceremonial office of vice president to get him out of state government and thus out of their hair. But Roosevelt wasn't quite the threat the moguls imagined him to be. He believed trusts were a necessary evil and agreed with John D. Rockefeller that the consolidation they promoted saved money wasted when companies competed. He did eventually attack those that he considered abusive, however, and Standard Oil was among them.

Other observers wanted all trusts reined in. A front-page headline in the *New York World* on March 11, 1901, read PRESIDENT HADLEY OF YALE UNIVERSITY MAKES A STARTLING PROPHECY. Speaking in Boston the night before, Hadley had said, "We shall have an emperor in Washington within twenty-five years unless we can provide a public sentiment which, regardless of legislation, will regulate the trusts."

In the late summer of 1901, President McKinley was assassinated and Roosevelt became president. Progressives were optimistic; Roosevelt was in some respects a reformer, favoring selective curbs on business. But Roosevelt was also careful to reassure businessmen.

In 1900, *McClure's* had lent aid to the reform movement by commissioning ex-convict Josiah Flynt Willard's "True Stories from the Underworld" and "The World of Graft." Willard's series describing police and official involvement in lawlessness in Boston, New York, and Chicago was crisp, frank, and shocking. In an editorial introducing it, Sam expressed his hope "that [the articles] will aid the movement now in progress to better the government of our cities." The crime rate in America had long fascinated him, and now he thought the cause was clear: corrupt politics.

Nothing like Willard's series had ever appeared in a national magazine before. Previously, *Harper's* and the *Century* had determined the subjects of conversation among the educated; their articles were "carefully drawn for a large, but not too large, audience that shaped cultural life." Their editors didn't hesitate to reject even great literature if it threatened middle-class sensibilities. But *McClure's* vanquished the belief that only an educated elite would support a reform-minded periodical.

Sam began changing those prudish cultural attitudes by encouraging writers like Willard. He and the others at *McClure's* wanted to tackle subjects like corruption so that they could write about "anything that interested

[them] — a state of bliss!" as Ray Stannard Baker put it. Other upsetting topics *McClure's* was considering included the death or maiming of more than 500,000 factory and industrial workers a year, twelve-hour shifts for young children in factories, tuberculosis-infected canned meat, and the open sale of votes.

Maurice Low, a British economist, wrote to Ida suggesting that *McClure's* run a series on a business trust, describing how it was set up, how it affected labor, what its political strategies were, and how its shares were traded on Wall Street. While Ida and Phillips found the idea persuasive, neither one

Sam McClure and an unknown companion on the deck of an ocean liner.

liked Low very much, and they agreed he was not the person to write such a series.

Efforts by federal and state governments to rein in trusts had been ineffectual but continued to make headlines. Standard Oil lawyers were nimbly developing ways to get around new regulations. Since Rockefeller usually had "forgotten" the facts when he was subpoenaed to testify before some commission or other, speculation about what he was really up to was rampant.

McClure felt that the public saw the menace in trusts but knew too little about them. He wrote Phillips from London: "The great feature is trusts. That will be the great question. . . . That will be the great, red-hot event. And the magazine that puts [out] the various phases of the subject that people want to be informed about will be bound to have a good circulation." John H. Finley attended a conference on trusts organized in Chicago by reformers Jane Addams (the founder of Hull House) and Woodrow Wilson. Sam eagerly awaited his report.

Convinced after weeks of debate that trusts was their subject, Ida and the staff in New York tried to decide which trust to focus on. Meanwhile, Sam suffered another nervous collapse. He checked in to Johns Hopkins with a high fever and was told to go abroad when he was well enough to travel and stay away for at least a year.

Ida visited him in the hospital on her way to Washington to gather material on the steel trust. Steel was under consideration for the series because the subject was timely; J. P. Morgan had only just founded U.S. Steel, the first billion-dollar corporation. But in the end, Ida couldn't figure out a way to make the story readable. It clearly didn't excite her imagination. Low had suggested investigating the sugar trust; however, she and Sam agreed that

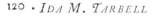

it likewise lacked the earth-shattering quality they needed. Baker proposed writing a piece about the recent discovery of oil in California. Ida rejected the idea as not a *McClure's* subject. Sam left for Europe with the question unresolved.

Ida replied to Baker that they needed a new plan of attack, a way to show how men were "combining and controlling these resources . . . [to] give an idea of what is really going on, in an entirely fresh and novel way." She asked him to come up with another suggestion.

The exchange prompted Ida to reminisce aloud at staff meetings about her childhood experience in the oil fields. She had seen the birth of the oil industry firsthand; she remembered the early signs that Rockefeller was out to dominate the independents and the pain this had caused — as when her father had assumed his partner's debts after the man's suicide. In Paris, she had read reformer Henry D. Lloyd's *Wealth Against Commonwealth,* whose villain was Rockefeller's Standard Oil monopoly. Her attempt to turn the story of Pithole into a novel while on the *Chautauquan* staff still lay in a drawer back in Titusville. She and her brother, Will, had gone back to Pithole in 1894 to see what was left. They failed to find even a trace of what had been a thriving town of 20,000. Will was now an executive of the only oil consortium that had defied the octopus.

Listening to Ida, Phillips realized that her life experience, along with her writerly and scholarly skills, uniquely equipped her to tell the story of the Standard Oil Trust — the mother of all trusts, they agreed, the only one created by a single man. When Phillips pointed this out, Ida reluctantly consented to take it on. After all, the material was probably all in the public record. She would just have to comb through it, numbing as that prospect was. Anyway, she always enjoyed the hunt for clues that led to more clues, to pyramiding discoveries, the great sifting, weighing, and interpreting that was research.

To launch the project, they needed Sam's approval. He was still in Europe with his wife, Hattie, the children, their nanny, a man to take care of their bicycles, and several nurses. Ida sailed in September 1901, expecting to stay in Lausanne for about a week, but she "hadn't reckoned with the McClure method." Her arrival elated Sam. Suddenly he was revived, bursting with ideas for their mutual entertainment. "I want a good time!" he declared. They would all travel to Greece via the Italian lakes and Venice and spend the winter there while he thought over the proposal. Ida had no choice but to go along.

When they got to Milan, Sam suddenly decided he and Hattie needed a cure before Greece and headed for the ancient watering place of Salsomaggiore. There they soaked in steam and wallowed in mud baths. For part of every day, Ida and Sam, sometimes bundled in blankets on a terrace overlooking the lake, chewed over plans for the story. Surprisingly, Sam was able to make up his mind on the spot. The Standard Oil Trust was their subject! A series about it would accomplish what they wished: to "give a notion of the process by which a particular industry passed from the control of the many to that of the few." McClure thought Ida should use the biographical approach she had found so effective in the past. Indeed, Rockefeller was a Napoleon of industry.

Now that Ida had a feature to write, Sam released her from going on to Greece. She returned to New York to begin work on what she still worried was "a doubtful enterprise for a magazine like *McClure's*." Would readers really enjoy a description of the web of interlocking corporations and their balance sheets? The magazine's last big feature had been the juicy undercover crime piece. Well, she would see.

In hindsight, Ida recalled that people tended to give *McClure's* credit for its courage in daring to investigate Rockefeller. But "courage implies a suspicion of danger. Nobody thought of such a thing in our office. . . . We were . . . only journalists intent on discovering what had gone into the making of this most perfect of monopolies. What had we to be afraid of?"

 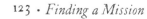

PART TWO

Achievement

CHAPTER TWELVE

Muckrakers Together

ONCE IDA HAD started working on "The History of the Standard Oil Company" early in 1902, she was too busy to function as desk editor of *McClure's*. Sam hired a young man to replace her, but the newcomer didn't sit behind a desk for long. Young, handsome, self-possessed Lincoln Steffens was a newspaperman from California. He was only five and a half feet tall, wore a pince-nez and natty clothes, and impressed many as cynical. The magazine sent him to report on city government in Cleveland. He would move on to other cities and write of widespread corruption, producing seminal articles that ran alongside Ida's.

Lincoln Steffens.

Ida came to regard Steffens as the most brilliant member of the staff. She said of him, "He was the least talkative of us all, observant rather than garrulous, the best listener in the group, save Mr. Phillips. [He] began his career . . . with an immense curiosity as to what was going on about him. Incredibly outspoken, taking rascality for granted, apparently never shocked or angry or violent, [he] coolly determined to demonstrate to men and women of good will and honest purpose what they were up against and warn them."

Their regard was mutual. Steffens recalled that when a squabble broke out among the *McClure's* writers, "it might have caused trouble had not Miss Ida M. Tarbell made peace, as she so often did thereafter. Sensible, capable, and very affectionate, she knew each of us and all our idiosyncrasies and troubles. She had none of her own so far as we ever heard. When we were deadlocked, we might each of us send for her and down she would come to the office, smiling, like a tall, good-looking young mother to say, 'Hush children.'"

Albert Boyden.

More convincingly, Steffens thought Ida the best journalist at *McClure's* and the only one besides himself who was easy to get along with. "She was another fellow — a nice fellow — we didn't have a feeling of man or woman in that office. There was never any doubt of her copy. It was so reliable, always on time, the rest of us were all unreliable."

Further expanding the staff, Ida hired Albert Boyden, a recent Harvard graduate, as production manager. His immense good cheer and capacity for friendship made him everyone's favorite. Ida loved the rollicking parties at Bert's apartment, which he shared with another young man. There were arguments over books, current events, and gossip, and Ida even kicked up her heels and danced. She and Bert grew very close. While she always addressed Phillips in person and on paper as Mr. Phillips, Boyden was frequently, from the start, "Dear Bert."

———— ❋ ————

In the years following the oil wars of 1872, John D. Rockefeller had become one of the richest men in America, owing his success to his paradoxical "tight-fisted control of details and advocacy of unbridled expansion." He controlled the production and distribution of oil in America and beyond. By building a business that dominated every aspect of oil production, delivery, and use, he had essentially invented the modern corporation.

The oil industry continued its dizzying rise and fall. Rockefeller was contemptuous of the small fry who entered it expecting to get rich quickly. He ridiculed his opponents, many of whom *were* feckless, making it easy for him to hoodwink them. Rockefeller, on the other hand, could comprehend the oil business as a whole and envision what it might become. He was canny, patient, and bold.

Companies were forbidden by law to grow across state boundaries, so he designed the trust to unite the companies he acquired or founded in various places. He offered cash or Standard Oil stock when buying out the independents and was confounded by the many timid managers who foolishly chose the cash option. Those who did accept stock eventually found themselves wealthy. Rockefeller referred to his "Godlike" company as "the angel of mercy" or "Moses." He claimed he disdained men who devoted all their waking hours to making money for money's sake. Even so, he kept expanding his business, seizing every opportunity and asserting that the company was forced to extend itself to every part of the world.

In an effort to dominate every stage of refining and distributing oil, Rockefeller bought tank cars, then pipelines, and finally banks and real estate. When competitors fought back, he bribed politicians to encourage favorable legislation and invested in newspapers so he could plant admiring stories about his company. When, in 1879, hearings into his monopoly arrangements with the railroads were conducted in New York, he became a fugitive from subpoenas and indictments, skittering between New York and Ohio. If he was compelled to testify, his answers were masterpieces of evasion; one headline read ROCKEFELLER IMITATES CLAM. When the court clerk swore him in, he would "kiss the Bible vehemently," as had his father before him. His demeanor radiated unconcern, but to calm his nerves he gnawed sticks of celery. No one ever saw him relax his self-control, even when one congressional committee called the SIC "the most gigantic and daring conspiracy against the free market ever conceived."

In 1881, reformer Henry Demarest Lloyd published an article in the *Atlantic Magazine* dissecting Standard Oil's monopoly. Lloyd pointed out that consumers were forced to pay higher prices when competition was stifled. Ida would also emphasize this point, making her investigation personally relevant to thousands of households. Referring to the bribery of officials, Lloyd wrote that Standard Oil had "done everything to the Pennsylvania legislature except to refine it."

Rockefeller never responded to criticisms or investigations, but he began giving money away in the 1890s. He endowed the University of Chicago, bailed out many old friends and colleagues to the tune of millions of dollars, and — despite, or maybe because of, his infamy — received nonstop appeals from the general public, which he ignored. According to his advisor on philanthropy, he was "constantly hunted, stalked and hounded almost like a wild animal." Even his father, who had assumed the alias Dr. Levingston, showed up occasionally to borrow money from his son, but the visits were kept secret. When Rockefeller's mother died, she was described in the press as a widow.

American oil was assumed to be confined to the depths below certain Pennsylvania counties, and Rockefeller's advisors feared it might run out. Standard Oil had customers around the world and needed oil to sell to them. Some of the trust's executives urged the company to drill in other places. New oil reserves were discovered in Ohio in 1885 — revealed to Rockefeller, he believed, by God — and Standard Oil expanded into that region. The new oil's sulfur content made it smell so horrible that some thought it useless, but Rockefeller promoted it for use as fuel. Standard Oil invested millions in the Ohio range, and by the 1890s Ohio had become the company's primary source of oil.

Standard Oil had conquered the refining market; now it was also the dominant producer of oil in the United States. Rockefeller persuaded his directors to keep investing by throwing millions of his own dollars into the enterprise. To destroy those independent producers who remained, Standard Oil ruthlessly undercut their prices and lured their customers away. Standard Oil also paid employees of independent companies to provide information that would help crush those independents. In the international marketplace, Standard Oil men spread rumors that Russian kerosene wasn't safe. Bribery and sabotage were also in the Standard Oil arsenal.

In 1890, the Sherman Antitrust Act, intended to rein in monopolistic practices, was passed. Rockefeller was unconcerned. The law's vague language and loopholes ensured that it wouldn't be enforced. Ohio state law prohibited the control of shares in an Ohio company from New York City; when a suit was filed against Standard Oil in Ohio, the trust simply reorganized itself. New Jersey law permitted corporations to hold stock in other corporations, so Standard Oil of New Jersey was born, a front for what was actually a nationwide network of interlocking companies. Standard Oil had become a giant banking operation, controlling so much wealth that it was no longer subject to market fluctuations.

By the 1890s Americans had come to expect steady sources of lighting, even in remote areas. As a result, kerosene remained highly profitable even after Thomas A. Edison began promoting his electric light bulb in 1880. As late as 1900, more Americans used oil lamps than electric ones. Standard Oil manufactured 86 percent of that lamp oil. When the oil industry began to foresee the end of gas lighting, along came the automobile, bringing a potential demand for oil so huge that worry over inadequate reserves was revived — until more oil was found in California.

In 1892, independent oil man Lewis Emery, who had heroically battled Standard Oil for years, began laying pipeline from the Pennsylvania oil fields to the West Coast to serve a new alliance of stubborn independent producers. The railroads under Standard Oil's control harassed Emery's workmen, arranging for passing trains to spew scalding steam, boiling water, and burning coals on them. Standard Oil also cut kerosene prices, finally defeating three of the independent companies. One cooperative managed to survive: the Pure Oil Company, of which Will Tarbell, Ida's brother, was treasurer.

Contrary to expectations and to doctor's orders, Sam McClure didn't stay put in Europe for a year after meeting with Ida in Italy. He bounced back to the office before Thanksgiving 1901. An outline of a three-piece series on

Standard Oil had been finished in October; Sam hastened to announce it in the November issue.

Ida spent the 1901 Christmas holidays in Titusville, where she found the locals in "a persistent fog of suspicion and fear." Her father warned her not to write the articles. "Don't do it. They [Standard Oil interests] will ruin the magazine." At a party that winter in Washington, an executive of a bank controlled by Standard Oil took her aside and muttered darkly that "they" were concerned about her work. Ida brushed off the veiled threat and indignantly told him it made no difference to her.

Standard Oil had been investigated almost continuously since its inception, so Ida assumed that public records of lawsuits and hearings would be readily available. She knew she had to amass such evidence before approaching any Standard Oil executives or they would erect a blockade. Committees in the House of Representatives, the Hepburn Committee in New York, the Interstate Commerce Commission, and others had all issued reports on Standard Oil. Henry Demarest Lloyd's book *Wealth Against Commonwealth* provided a road map through this material, but she had to see it all for herself.

For Ida, the SIC episode of railroad price fixing and kickbacks was the centerpiece, and her own memory of it remained vivid. But when she began looking for documentation of Standard Oil's involvement in the SIC, the same people who had advised her to refrain from looking closely at the trust insisted that Standard Oil had destroyed all records of the episode. Ida refused to believe that. More sleuthing indicated that there were three extant copies of a pamphlet produced in 1873 called *The Rise and Fall of the South Improvement Company*, two in private collections. The owners refused to let her see them. Then a bibliographer at the New York Public Library told her that yes, heads of railroads had bought nearly every copy of the pamphlet and had them destroyed. But there was one left — in the library. Now Ida knew that when some piece of information was declared destroyed, it meant that she should keep looking for it.

She could prove that the SIC was the tool of Rockefeller. The pamphlet described how the railroads had agreed to provide tank cars and other equipment for oil shipping. The refiners had received rebates of up to 50 percent on their shipments as well as "drawbacks," a percentage of the money rival refiners had paid the railroads. Rockefeller had promised the conspiring railroads all his business in return for these exclusive terms. The practice was not actually illegal at the time, but it was certainly an underhanded and covert stifling of competition.

While Ida was in Cleveland, delving more deeply into the morass of Standard Oil's history there, Bert Boyden wrote her to complain that Sam's behavior was out of control. He was undermining the effectiveness of the staff. Ida sent an unruffled reply. "Things will turn out all right. The General may stir up things and interfere with the general comfort but he puts the health of life into the work at the same time. . . . When he's fussing and fretting and bothering you keep your eyes open, something is weak or wrong. He feels it and the rest of us are too preoccupied. . . . Never forget that it was he and nobody else who has created that place. You must learn to believe in him and *use* him if you are going to be happy there. He is an extraordinary creature. . . . Genius comes once in a generation and if you ever get in its vicinity thank the Lord and *stick*."

This was an extraordinary expression of Ida's tolerance for her boss's erratic ways. In the short term her faith was amply justified; when she turned in her first drafts of the Standard Oil articles, McClure rewarded her with a big block of company stock.

After the series was announced in November, Mark Twain asked Sam if

Ida would like to meet his friend Henry Rogers, a vice president of Standard Oil. Twain was profoundly grateful to Rogers, who had helped extricate him from crippling debts. It isn't clear whether Twain was transmitting an overture from Rogers or offering to be useful to his other friend, McClure. In any case, Ida leaped at the chance to penetrate Rockefeller's lair.

In 1861, Rogers and a friend had pooled some money, gone to the Pennsylvania oil region, and set up a refinery. Young Rogers spoke out against the SIC scheme. Before long, however, Rockefeller had persuaded Rogers and his partner, Charles Pratt, to sell out to his company. By the time that company had morphed into the Standard Oil Trust, Rogers was its number-three man, after John D. Rockefeller and his brother William.

Henry H. Rogers.

The virile, piratically mustachioed Rogers excited Ida's fervent regard. She described him as "handsomest, lithe as an Indian, sensitive nose, beautiful hair, mouth capable of both firm decision and gay laughter." Or perhaps she was merely sketching a character who would be irresistible to her readers. They began the first interview with formal reserve, and then the two discovered mutually gratifying memories of Rouseville in the 1870s that tempered their wariness. Rogers admitted that the SIC scheme had been a mistake but bragged of the trust's mighty achievements. He even promised to try to arrange an interview for Ida with John D. himself, but that never came to pass.

Standard Oil's headquarters in New York bore no name plaque, just an address, 26 Broadway, which was legendary. Ida visited Rogers there repeatedly over the course of two years. Her notes of their conversations filled nineteen pages, several of them transcripts of their bantering. Rogers was acting as a Standard Oil public relations spokesman. When they got down to business, each was controlled and civil. Once, Ida let loose and referred to a Standard Oil associate as a liar and a hypocrite. Rogers didn't engage, saying only, "I think it is going to rain."

Word that Ida was holding powwows at 26 Broadway traveled through oil circles. She paid a price for the interviews: assuming she was allied with Standard Oil, some of the independents refused to talk to her.

Visitors to 26 Broadway were prevented from seeing other visitors or anyone else on the way to their appointments. Ida was led along a different route each time she went, entering through one door and exiting by another, aware of a shadowy figure watching her. She, who earned $4,000 per article, learned that Rogers's secretary's annual salary was an awesome $10,000. With it came "that gleam of hardness that efficient business women rarely escape."

From Rogers she received insights into the human motives and justifications that fleshed out the information in the documents. He explained corporate decisions from the inside and produced records to illustrate them. Ida probed him about a Standard Oil subsidiary of which he was a director, which had been accused of sabotaging a rival's refinery in Buffalo. While she concluded from his responses that no sabotage had taken place, she was sure that Standard Oil had used espionage and other criminal means to eliminate its rival. But she couldn't prove it.

The breakthrough evidence finally came to her by an unexpected path. A Standard Oil office boy, charged with destroying records every night by burning them, happened to notice the name of his Sunday school teacher, who was a refiner by profession, on several of the documents destined for the fire. The papers showed that the railroads were warning Standard Oil of the refiner's shipments in advance. Standard Oil then shipped its product first, undercutting the independent. The boy took the papers to his teacher, who had read Ida's first installments and believed in her integrity, and who passed the evidence on to her. It was the proof Ida needed that Standard Oil was still practicing espionage and dirty tricks.

When *McClure's* published the documents in an installment titled "Cutting to Kill" in February 1904, Rogers asked her furiously, "Where did you get that stuff?" She countered, "You know very well that I could not tell you . . . but you know very well that it is authentic." This episode ended their connection. Rogers refused to meet with her again.

CHAPTER THIRTEEN

Siddall

$\mathcal{T}$HE FRUSTRATION OF searching courthouses, libraries, and archives for documents reported missing or destroyed convinced Ida that she needed an assistant, preferably an energetic, curious, smart college graduate with initiative. Late in the summer of 1901, she obtained the names of three candidates, all men, from newspaper editors in Cleveland and sent each of them a sample assignment.

The standout was John Siddall, a go-getter of twenty-seven, plump and boyish, who was on the staff of the *Chautauquan,* which was now based in Cleveland. As secretary of the board of education, Siddall was well connected in the city. Ida asked him, as his audition assignment, to find portraits of Rockefeller and early refiners. Siddall responded with enthusiasm, promising not only to follow instructions but also to make suggestions. Furthermore, his brother, a lawyer, represented Frank Rockefeller, one of John D.'s brothers, as well as an independent oil company. Ida replied that she knew he would exercise "all discretion," and she hoped the work was "something [he'd] be glad to have been associated with."

Siddall's sources warned him that he'd tackled a hopeless job: "Standard Oil had been deceived and maligned so often that none of its adherents will furnish one particle of aid to any publication in the land." He conveyed his doubts to the magazine's staff while Ida was away in Europe. Bert Boyden wrote to Siddall regretting that Siddall couldn't do the work — did he know of anyone else?

But Siddall didn't back out after all. He obtained photographs, including what he believed to be the

John Siddall.

only portrait of John D. Rockefeller from the 1870s. He found old books with other rare pictures, such as one published by the local YMCA. He ingratiated himself with local photographers and hunted through their old negatives. Ida sent him a list of refiners who had sold out in 1870–71 and had him check it for accuracy. There was also a list of those who had refused to give in. She enclosed two dollars for copying documents by hand. From time to time she asked for reassurance that he was being paid enough for his services, to confirm that one hundred dollars a month was reasonable.

Siddall understood from the start what Ida wanted. Like Charles Downer Hazen, he became a younger coconspirator whose outlook on the world was compatible with her own. Occasionally they met, spoke on the phone, or sent telegrams, but most of their collaboration was conducted by mail. Their correspondence is ironic, wry, sharp, and judgmental. When she completed an installment, she asked Siddall for "rigid" criticism. He gave it, asking for clarifications and improvements. But overall he was captivated by what Ida did with the material. "It's tremendous . . . it reads like a novel," he enthused.

After interviewing officials in Washington, combing through court documents, visiting libraries, using the files lent her by Henry D. Lloyd, and talking to oil men, Ida confessed to feeling overwhelmed. "There is so much hocus pocus about these matters," she told Siddall. She traveled to the oil regions in the West to hunt down clues. Once she took some documents home from Cleveland by mistake and joked, "I feel as if I had a package of dynamite in my small establishment!"

Rockefeller's rigid insistence on anonymity and evasion meant that details of his secret machinations were not to be found in his papers. He ruled his empire with "winks, nods and hints . . . never spelling anything out. His letters amounted to little more than cryptic notes. . . . He wrote as if to thwart any future investigators who might get hold of the documents."

The rest of the magazine's staff eagerly read "Sid's" letters. Sam and Phillips began talking about hiring him as soon as he was no longer needed in Cleveland.

The first installment of "The History of the Standard Oil Company" appeared in November 1902. Ida told the story of the discovery of oil, sketching characters and scenes, adding color to clear, concise technical description. She depicted the moment when George H. Bissell, having learned that oil could be put to practical use, realized how it could be pulled from the earth: "One day, walking down Broadway, he halted to rest in the shade of an awning before a drugstore. In the window he saw on a bottle a curious label, 'Kier's Petroleum, or Rock Oil' it read. . . . Produced from a well in Allegheny Co., Pa. four hundred feet below the earth's surface." On the label was a picture of an artesian well. It was from this well that Mr. Kier got his "natural remedy."

She portrayed the independent producers as innocents who had boldly risked everything in a precarious enterprise: "They came in shoals, young, vigorous, resolute, indifferent to difficulty, greedy for a chance, and each year they forced more light and wealth from a new product. . . . Suddenly, at

The opening page of Ida's history-making series.

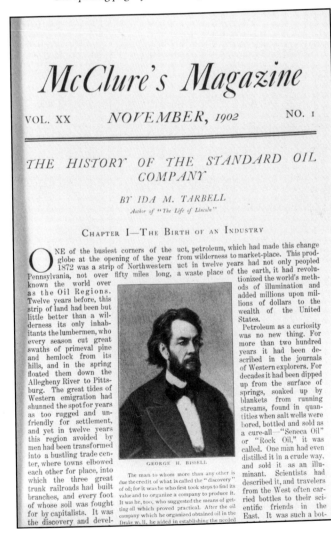

the very heyday of this confidence, a big hand reached out from they knew not where, to steal this conquest and throttle their future." Thus she laid the ground for Rockefeller's great betrayal.

When he received the third installment, Sam realized he had history-making revelations in his hands. He decided to run two parallel articles along with Ida's: Baker's investigation of labor violence in the coal industry, in which the United Mine Workers union was depicted as behaving like a trust, and Steffens's on corruption in municipal government. Sam's editorial for the January 1903 issue noted that all three pieces together amounted to "an arraignment of American character" and might have been titled "The American Contempt for Law."

Sam charged the clergy, colleges, judges, and lawyers with varying degrees of lawlessness. In every case, it was the public who paid for their carelessness and greed. He pointed out that the concentration of financial power in Wall Street was a growing threat to democratic institutions.

The threat of class warfare between economic interest groups had been growing since the 1880s. The responsible parties were all, in the end, members of the public. The time had come, Sam said, for the public to wake up and assume responsibility for the contempt for law running rampant in the land. He ended the editorial with a call to arms: "There is no one left: none but all of us. . . . The public is the people. . . . We have to pay in the end, every one of us. And in the end the sum total of the debt will be our liberty."

Although investigative journalism had been practiced for a long time, this issue of *McClure's,* its articles and the editorial, marked a seminal moment in what would later be called muckraking. Sam's editorial laid out the process: Investigative journalists exposed the problem; the citizenry read about it and mobilized to demand change. Sam was thrilled by the impact of what amounted to a crusade. Circulation of his magazine didn't match its high of 1900, but the January 1903 issue sold out at once. Other magazines eagerly jumped on the bandwagon, commissioning their own exposés. Most important, someone in the White House at last took an interest: President Roosevelt sent Ida a note of congratulation.

Siddall's excitement was palpable as he discovered evidence that Standard Oil had begun manipulating market prices in 1876, when the independents had staged a comeback. Ida wrote to him that she would use a memo written by SIC cofounder Henry Flagler, boasting that raising the price of a barrel just a quarter of a cent would net them millions, to prove that the company's aim was always to artificially prop up consumer prices.

"The History of the Standard Oil Company" contrasted the SIC executives' scheme of rebates and drawbacks with the position of the independents, who, Ida contended, welcomed competition. In a key episode, a woman known as the Widow Backus was bullied into selling her lubricating plant for less than it was worth. A few years later, Rockefeller defended himself against the charge that he had forced her to sell cheap: "I regret that Mrs. Backus did not take at least part of her pay in Standard certificates [stock] as we suggested she should do."

Ida described Standard Oil's takeover of a pipeline developed by independents, the espionage employed by Standard Oil against its competitors, the supposed sabotage of a Buffalo refinery by Rogers and associates, and finally, the rigged election of an Ohio "senator from Standard Oil."

But Ida also found herself disillusioned by her heroes, the independents. She wrote to Siddall, "As the work goes on I am perfectly amazed at the way it develops. . . . My wrath at the independents is growing as great as my wrath at the Standard. They seem always to have flunked at the critical moment." Nevertheless, she kept her sights trained on the octopus and what she saw as an unfair fight.

Ida seized on the hypocrisy of Rockefeller's making donations to his church in the 1880s while at the same time forcing smaller competitors out of business. This was the sort of detail that made the story dramatic. "It would be interesting psychologically too," she wrote, "to know if he really healed his conscience by helping the 'Church of the Holy Blue Barrel,'" i.e., Standard Oil, which shipped its product in blue containers.

One day Siddall excitedly reported that John D.'s father, a.k.a. Dr. Levingston, was still alive. "Old Dr. Rockefeller is 92 years old, living in Tipton, Iowa . . . John has no use for him." Siddall's source reported that at a family reunion in Cleveland the old man told dirty stories and swore, to the disgust of his son. Ida revealed the old man's existence in an installment, but she was never able to discover his whereabouts. When Joseph Pulitzer, publisher of the *World,* read in *McClure's* that old Rockefeller was alive, he offered to pay $8,000 to anyone who could locate him. The result was a nationwide manhunt that failed to find him.

Ida thought she could perceive character from faces and became obsessed with the idea of laying eyes on John D. Rockefeller in the flesh. She asked Siddall repeatedly to find a recent photograph of him. Siddall recruited friends to identify themselves as Rockefeller relatives and ask Cleveland photography studios to search their files. Once he sent a man with a camera to pose as a Sunday school teacher at a Rockefeller church picnic. These ruses failed to capture a portrait of the retiring mogul, who hated publicity and probably hated his own appearance as well. A disease had caused all of his hair to fall out. Ironically, his elusiveness only worsened his reputation.

In June 1903, Siddall slipped into the church where Rockefeller "was warding off the devil for another week" during a service. Rockefeller handed out envelopes of money to the needy. "Doesn't this shake your belief in the theory of pure hypocrisy?" Siddall asked Ida.

"I am much anxious to know what sort of a mouth he was developing in those years," Ida replied. Rockefeller's mouth was concealed by a mustache in early photographs. Ida was more eager than ever to have an up-to-date portrait to enhance the series. Did they dare send a brave photographer to the Cleveland church?

In the meantime, Ida and Siddall collected evidence of Rockefeller's good works as well as the many black marks on his character. He had kept his old house in Cleveland open so that the servants would have a place to live. This unpublicized gesture seemed to Ida more genuinely benevolent than Rockefeller's increasingly famous donations to charities, which she considered mostly hypocritical.

In July, Ida took a vacation, joining the McClures at Divonne-les-Bains, a spa near Geneva, Switzerland. Sam was entangled with Florence Wilkinson, a comely young poet whose verses he had been publishing — indeed, more frequently than those of any other poet. When Hattie McClure went alone to Paris to shop, Sam took Miss Wilkinson to Chamonix, where he arranged adjoining rooms for them overlooking Mont Blanc. On the voyage home, Sam commemorated his and Hattie's anniversary by presenting his wife with a ring set with precious gems and a cake bedecked with flags and candles. Looking on, Ida worried about the implications of Sam's relationship with Miss Wilkinson for the magazine and for her own future.

Back home, Henry Lloyd, who had written about the Standard Oil monopoly two decades before, was now willing to meet with Ida, although he had earlier put her off. He told her that rebates were still being awarded to shippers, who destroyed the evidence. He called Rockefeller and company examples of "the most dangerous tendencies in modern life." She borrowed his files and drew on them for her own articles.

By the fall of 1904, Ida and Siddall still hadn't found an up-to-date image of Rockefeller. Without one, the series would be incomplete. They decided on a radical plan. The only place Rockefeller ever appeared in public was his church. She and Siddall would sneak into it, incognito. Phillips suggested they take along a sketch artist. Dreading exposure, Siddall enlisted some friends tall enough to shield himself and Ida from view.

The group slunk into the Sunday school room where Rockefeller began every Sabbath morning. They attracted no notice. When Rockefeller walked in, Ida reflected afterward, he looked like "the oldest man I had ever seen . . . but what power!" He swung his reptilian head from side to side, scanning the room, agitated and, Ida concluded, fearful. She found herself feeling sorry for him, assuming he was tormented by a guilty conscience. Her curiosity about his mouth was finally satisfied: It was just a slit, without lips.

Rockefeller, sketched by the artist Varian during Ida's infiltration of the Sunday school.

Robber barons were accustomed to operating without regard for public opinion. Privately, Rockefeller expressed anger at "my lady friend" or "Miss Tarbarrel." He and his wife and two of his daughters fell ill with one ailment or another while the articles were being published. His son John D. Rockefeller Jr. seemed to suffer most from the opprobrium that followed Ida's exposé. He had a nervous breakdown and decamped to Europe for two years. When John D. Sr. published his autobiography in 1911, it was to justify everything Standard Oil had done. He chided his readers, "Do you think that this trade has been developed by anything but hard work?"

The Periodical Publishers Association held their annual dinner in the spring of 1904. President Roosevelt, Secretary Taft, the French and German ambassadors, a few senators, and the entire staff of *McClure's* were there — all but Ida, their star. It was a stag party. "It is the first time since I came into the office that the fact of petticoats has stood in my way," she wrote to Baker dryly, "and I am half inclined to resent it."

As the magazine published damning piece after damning piece with no rebuttal from Rockefeller, Ida's colleagues urged her to follow up with a character sketch, which appeared in 1905. In it, she summarized Rockefeller's early life and origins, identifying the SIC episode as the point at which Rockefeller made the fateful choice between good and evil — and paid the price for it in lifelong paranoia and stomach troubles. Ida allowed herself searing descriptions, justified by the "menace" of the kind of business Rockefeller had founded. He had helped to arouse "the most universal and powerful passion in this country — the passion for money." His business dealings, charitable works, and private life were all of a piece. She told her readers that a man with Rockefeller's influence could not be permitted to "live in the dark." His philanthropies, for example, were not simple good works; they gave him enormous influence over which aspects of American life would thrive.

Soberly and relentlessly, she totted up his sins and asked, "Why does he do it? Why does he want an income of $25,000,000 and more? . . . So far as the world knows, he is poor in his pleasures. . . . His bequests are small compared to his wealth. . . . Rockefeller is the victim of a money-passion which blinds him to every other consideration in life, which is stronger than his sense of justice, his humanity, his affections, his joy in life, which is the tyrannous, insatiable force of his being. 'Money-mad, money-mad. Sane in every other way, but money-mad,' was the late Senator [Mark] Hanna's comment on Rockefeller. And the late Senator Hanna could not be accused of holding money in light regard." She even found fault with the design and decor of Rockefeller's houses. But he was deemed a praiseworthy husband and father and an admirable believer in everyday economies, compared to other tycoons.

Rockefeller at the time of Ida's scathing "character sketch."

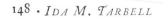

Opening Part 2 of the sketch, Ida went after Rockefeller's wizened face. The magazine had found a formal photograph and reproduced both a drawing made from it and the sketch from the church escapade. She invited readers to study the images. They presented "concentration, craftiness, cruelty and something indefinably repulsive." He was "a living mummy," stealthy and secretive. "There is probably not a public character whose private life is more completely concealed than that of John D. Rockefeller."

Rockefeller hid himself within a "cult of the unpretentious." He had no feeling for aesthetics, she observed, but he loved fresh air and played golf so often the game was thought to keep him from "completing his ownership of the nation." But "if Mr. Rockefeller played golf purely for pleasure," Ida wrote, "then those who fear him might indeed cease to worry . . . there is little doubt that Mr. Rockefeller's chief reason for playing golf is that he may live longer in order to make more money."

Ida described Rockefeller's father's career as a quack and a con man. She revealed that William Avery Rockefeller had been indicted for horse theft and rape. *McClure's* had managed to find a picture of "Doc" Rockefeller and printed it along with Ida's character sketch of his son. Residents of Freeport, Illinois, recognized the individual pictured as their neighbor Dr. Levingston and wrote to *McClure's* that there must be some mistake. No one, however, followed through; "Doc" Rockefeller, a.k.a. Dr. Levingston, was still incognito when he died in 1906. One of Ida's sources for venomous stories about John D. Rockefeller was his envious brother Frank, who, despite having borrowed hundreds of thousands from his brother, planned to publish his own mudslinging biography. He petitioned Ida to ghostwrite it, but she declined.

How did Ida manage to dig up and explain the deliberately obscured and concealed methods of the trust? She was a markedly patient, skeptical, and persevering investigator, and she had a cunning and tireless helper in Siddall. Even so, it is hard to see how she could have done it had she not been a witness to Standard Oil's beginnings and been invited into Henry Rogers's inner sanctum. Ida's achievement is reflected in Sam's admiring words: "The way you are generally esteemed and reverenced pleases me tremendously. You are today the most generally famous woman in America. You have achieved a great distinction. People universally speak of you with such reverence that I am getting sort of afraid of you."

Ida is caricatured fanning the flames of her exposé to smoke the unresponsive Rockefeller out of his hiding place.

Rockefeller could have challenged some of the evidence Ida cited, but he didn't — partly out of arrogance, but also because disputing the few things she might have gotten wrong would have implied that the rest of her account was true. Ida's series provoked editorials and sermons all over the nation but nary a word from Rockefeller or the trust.

In fact, Rockefeller did have the means to ruin *McClure's* — his operatives might have pressured advertisers to abandon it, undermining Ida's reputation. But he was probably certain that the web of secrecy that was his business method protected Standard Oil from unwanted exposure.

It fell to Elbert Hubbard, self-promoting founder of the Ryecroft Colony in upstate New York, to challenge Ida in a pamphlet, five million copies of which were purchased and distributed to the press, teachers, and ministers by Standard Oil in 1910. Hubbard wrote, "Ida Tarbell is an honest, bitter, talented, prejudiced and disappointed woman who wrote from her own point of view. And that point of view is in the ditch where her father's wheelbarrow was landed by a Standard Oil tank wagon. . . . She shot from cover and she shot to kill." The *Oil City Derrick* (which became a Standard Oil supporter after Rockefeller invested in it) ran a story headed "Hysterical Woman Versus Historical Fact." But the shocking impact of Ida's indictment was not blunted.

Ida condemned Standard Oil's methods, but did not reject capitalism itself: "I was willing that they should combine and grow as big and rich as they could but only by legitimate means." She found "legitimate greatness" that was tarnished by dishonest practices: "There was not a lazy bone in the organization nor an incompetent hand, nor a stupid head. They had never played fair, and that ruined their greatness for me."

In the early days of the oil industry, no one was blameless. The independents accepted rebates when offered them. They entered into agreements that stifled competition. They fought Rockefeller with compacts of their own. But Ida saw the conflict in black and white. After the articles were published in book form, the press adopted the cynical view that Rockefeller's philanthropies were intended to distract the public from his misdeeds.

It is staggering, in the Internet age, to realize how much criminal activity and corruption was successfully hidden from public view at the turn of the twentieth century. According to one veteran newsman, *McClure's* exposed trusts, gangs, political bosses, vice rackets, and corruption, but above all "exposed our lack of a national journalism." Ray Stannard Baker claimed that "[the] ignorance [of citizens] causes most of our problems." *McClure's* came through, with long, complex, well-researched, and intelligently argued articles. Americans in an era without radio, television, or the Internet read them with keen interest. So did the government. In 1906, the U.S. attorney general began to prosecute Standard Oil under the Sherman Antitrust Act.

CHAPTER FOURTEEN

An Unhinged Boss

I N 1904 A ROOM had been set aside at the McClure residence in Ardsley, a few miles north of New York City, for Ida to use on weekends. Sam wrote to Hattie, "In buying things for Miss Tarbell's room I want you to know that I told her you were planning to make her a nice home there. Miss Tarbell did us a great service the last two or three years. . . . In case of my death she would be your mainstay as Mr Phillips doesn't realize other peoples unreliability & I shall be away a lot next year and you will enjoy having her out."

Ida visited Ardsley while she was working on the Standard

Sam McClure at the height of his success.

153

Oil articles and was able to observe the McClure marriage at close range. She was fond of Hattie and hoped that Sam would master his amorous inclinations. If his relationship with the poet Florence Wilkinson became more than a short-lived flirtation, it could jeopardize the magazine as well as his marriage.

Sam McClure's grandson, in his biography of his grandfather, expressed doubt that a full-blown affair existed. In his view, Sam's willingness to hire women workers meant that he was "surrounded by spinsters," and the uproar that erupted over Miss Wilkinson was a symptom of their hysteria. The woman who ran the London office may well have sounded hysterical when she wrote to Ida that their lovesick editor was "degenerate, bloated, polluted, disfigured with vice, and incurable." But John Phillips, an unflappable male, also found cause for alarm.

In May 1904 Miss Wilkinson submitted a poem to the magazine that contained these lines: "I took you into my lonely arms; / You were the soul of me; / There was no speech between us twain, / There needed not be." The magazine's staff wondered privately if this was a love note to the editor. When Sam ordered his letter accepting the poem for publication to be delivered to its author along with an armload of flowers, Ida, Phillips, and Boyden rushed to confront him. He admitted he had written incriminating letters to Miss Wilkinson.

Ida was appalled. If the letters were leaked to some gossip sheet or rival publisher, they could destroy the *McClure's* legacy. Her reputation and financial interests were inseparable from the magazine's; her only savings were in the magazine's stock.

Phillips hurried to Wilkinson's apartment and extracted her promise to return Sam's letters. She offered to send any future correspondence to Sam in care of his wife! "Is there an epidemic of lunacy? . . . My small nephew used the word 'bughouse' this morning. It expresses my feelings," wrote Phillips to Ida.

"My Dear Mr. Phillips," Ida replied. "The Lord help us! *I'm* too small for this! There is nothing for us, I should say, but to keep a stern and unrelenting front. Evidently Mrs. McC is not to be counted on for that. Letters under her convoy! He can persuade her to do anything and if in the end we see a *menage à troi*s [three-person household], I shall not be greatly surprised. But that wouldn't last. He would soon want another! He's . . . an uncivilized, immoral, untutored natural man with enough canniness to keep himself out of jails and asylums. He is not to be trusted and I rather think our only hope is in Miss Wilkinson."

The crisis had drawn Ida and Phillips closer. She wrote Bert Boyden that they were dining together and getting to be almost "easy in one another's presence! He is certainly the rarest — most beautiful soul on earth." And, she noted, "he has to pay for his qualities in suffering and loneliness," referring to Sam's inconstancy as friend and partner and the long hours Phillips had to spend working, away from his family.

Sam breezily assured his team that he was "all right" and declared, "I've been an awful fool. My desires and my duties again jump together." He and Hattie went to Europe to repair their union. But there was less hope of repairing trust in the office. Before long, Hattie reappeared there, having been sent home by Sam to look after his interests. She apologetically told Phillips that she felt "it would goad him into violent madness" if she didn't do what he asked. She had stopped in London on her way to confide in a friend. Sam was her youngest child, she admitted to her friend, the "heart of my heart." But he was "long used to living on excitement."

Sam, too, soon materialized in New York, claiming to be a new man. Ida found him unchanged. "While he talked his mind was by jerks on something else. . . . He is still the same canny, scheming, unstable soul." She added that she had hardly the energy to care what he was up to.

As editor, Sam was still capable of rallying the troops. He called a staff meeting to remind them that the magazine was like the work of an artist. Art was not created to be sold, but to express the creator's "notion." When *McClure's* veered from expressing its notion by putting sales first, it lost its mission like an actor who became popular and felt he must live up to his fame by hamming. The magazine must not succumb to self-consciousness, Sam insisted. It existed solely as a medium for interesting reading.

This was a sound, even profound assessment. But cracks in the edifice were pulling the structure down. The landmark January 1903 issue had sold out, but the syndicate was losing money and so was the book-publishing arm. Those who sneered that Sam had gone cynically into publishing exposés to make circulation rise were mistaken. He hadn't, and it hadn't.

Sam's head hurt, his abdomen was "tired," and he couldn't sleep. Hattie suspected he was still pursuing other women. She wondered to Phillips if she should have her husband committed to an asylum. In the spring of 1905 Sam's current doctor ordered him to hasten back to Europe.

Ida, Boyden, and Phillips had lost all faith in their boss. Ida dreaded the next manifestation of Sam's madness. She couldn't help but feel compassion for him: he was ill and needed her protection. Sam suspected the change in her feelings. He sent her a conciliatory note: "I have always cared for you in a special manner, as much as a man can care for a woman without loving her."

Sam's amorous misadventures came to a head in the summer, when Hattie brought Ida a manuscript titled "The Shame of S. S. McClure." Given to Hattie by its author, Edith Wherry, for publication in the magazine, it recounted Sam's dalliance with Wherry. Phillips managed to suppress the manuscript. The file Ida kept on Sam's indiscretions (labeled "L'affaire") contains a page describing the Wherry manuscript, with the following observation: "500–1000 note — good businesswoman! Second thousand since May to my knowledge 1000 returned at C."

The meaning of that notation can only be guessed at, but one possible conclusion is that Wherry was engaged in successful extortion.

Sam swore that his infatuations were over, and this time Ida believed him. His new enthusiasms were all editorial: he wanted a series on the life insurance industry and another on railroads. The magazine seemed to be back to normal.

———— ✳ ————

Ida had the attention of millions, including the president, who commissioned his own investigation of Standard Oil. The book made from her Standard Oil articles was adapted in 1905 as a hit Broadway play called *The Lion and the Mouse*. Ida was offered the role of the heroine, with a salary of $2,500 a week for twenty weeks, the highest sum an actress had been offered to date. Unsurprisingly, she refused. The popular humorist Finley Peter Dunne, whose persona was that of a comic Irishman, referred to "Idarem [Ida M.] on Jawn D" in one of his columns, and Idarem became her office nickname.

In 1905, Ida's father died of gastric cancer. She was devastated. To try to lighten that darkness, she bought and confided in another little journal. "There has come a point when it is life or death-in-life and I am not willing to give up life. . . . If the innermost recesses are to be entered I must go there alone. I am conscious so much of myself is evading me, and this poor little book is a feeble prop in my effort to reach land I've never explored," she wrote. She had hoped to find solace in introspection, but she didn't know the way. Self-examination felt immodest. She was suffering an emotional

Ida, Esther, and Sarah mourning Franklin in Titusville, 1905.

crisis, but she was too busy surviving it to indulge in soul-searching. If she ever recorded any insights, it was on the pages she then razored out.

Her father's death, the turmoil at work, and sudden, unbidden notoriety left Ida in a vulnerable state. Work was always her one real cure for self-pity and regret. Although she was "fifty, fagged, wanting to be left alone," Ida plunged into the oil controversy in Kansas, where independent producers were fighting off Standard Oil and officials were trying to make oil a publicly owned resource. Ida later called it the most exciting trip she had ever made, although her new reputation was something of a burden. She told Bert Boyden, "They take me too seriously. Every time I make a move it goes into the papers."

One day she drove in a buckboard across the state line to stay briefly in Tulsa, in Oklahoma Territory. The next morning she was informed that local settlers wanted to serenade her and expected a speech in return. The prospect of addressing them horrified her, so she sent someone to buy a box of cigars and passed them around to the all-male crowd instead. An Indian offered her a compliment she especially cherished: "He all right."

Ida had made the Kansas controversy a national issue. After soliciting her opinion of his arguments, the new Missouri attorney general filed suit to have Standard Oil's licenses revoked. It was rumored that Rockefeller left the country to avoid testifying.

Back in 1900, Ida had received an unexpected announcement from Charles Downer Hazen, who had become a professor of history at Smith College. They had met from time to time in the years after Paris and exchanged humorous, affectionate, and fairly uninhibited letters, given the era's starchy proprieties. Now Hazen wrote, "The worst has happened and your faith in me is severely tested. I am engaged to Miss Sally Duryea of New York and I am very exultant over that fact." Having broken their agreement to avoid marriage, he hoped Ida would "approve my apostasy." Hazen clearly understood that his news would, at the very least, disappoint her. But Ida managed to say she was happy for him. Her life had changed even more than his had. They could both move on, their friendship altered but secure.

On May 7, 1905, she made the first entry in her journal since the day, overcome by grief for her father, she had bought it: "If I could follow the

experience of the last few days — follow it and catch it — and hold it — and put it into words I would be better acquainted with myself. It is my Henry James experience."

Famed novelist James had returned to the States for a lecture tour after living for twenty years in Europe. Ida had developed a jumble of powerful, unexamined feelings about him, although she had never met him. A few months earlier, his portrait had come into her hands. She searched the "wise, sensitive[,] unattainable" face for signs of his character, as she had searched Rogers's and then Rockefeller's, but with very different results. She recognized "comprehension" in James's "great visage." She wanted to be understood by one so "big and wise and sweet." Although she had "hardly read his writings," she fixed upon James as "a soul to sit by as one does by a cathedral." "I let its [the portrait's] power filter in, and then I wrote the Hazens I wanted to spend a Sunday with them." It isn't clear whether she knew that Henry James would be there.

Henry James.

Hazen responded with an invitation to a dinner to be given for James in Northampton, Massachusetts. Ida was overcome by a sense of her own "rudeness, ignorance, inartisteness." She "blushed" to think of "sitting near

[James]." Still, she very much wanted to go, for she was sure that James held something she needed. So she accepted the invitation, then lay awake nights, dreading the occasion.

In Northampton, finding herself at last in James's presence, Ida was tongue-tied. She adoringly observed him from the end of the table while taking note of another guest's fatuous babbling. Struggling with shyness, she had "leaped another peak when he looked at [her] and called [her] name," and asked herself, "Why? Vanity — is it? To know that after all there is something in this poor thing I've been trying to foster — of a recognition. Let me say here for myself — It is a thirst for justification for an assurance I'm on the right road. I'm real as far as I go. I live a sham. . . . I wanted to be assured. How pitiful I am." She was afraid that James might have found her work on Standard Oil unworthy. Outwardly, Ida would have seemed composed. Her inward turmoil and womanly self-consciousness utterly unsettled her.

The following day James gave a lecture titled "The Lesson of Balzac." It was his insight that the great nineteenth-century French novelist had the "felt sense of life," that his characters existed "independently of their creator." He claimed that "there is no such thing in the world as an adventure pure and simple; there is only mine and yours, and his and hers — it being the greatest adventure of all, I verily think, just to be you or I, just to be he or she."

Ida thought his talk contained the greatest literary criticism she had ever heard. It penetrated her soul: "I see it and there is the lesson I've got to learn — to comprehend all — to wade boldly into life and yet never let the thing — the experience — engulf you. To keep always the mastery of it — that you may interpret life." James had identified for her the great balancing act of existence — to thoroughly engage in an authentic way, yet never lose her grip, never be led off center.

She complimented James after the lecture, and he said (she underlined the words in her journal), *"I hope you are planning to be around these two or three days, Miss!"* Hazen took James home afterward and later reported to Ida that he had called her work on Standard Oil "great." He had added, "She has a *striking* personality." Hearing this, Ida wrote, "This is the barest I have ever stripped myself."

The next day, she and Hazen went for a long ride. Perhaps they spoke about how their friendship had been affected by his marriage. "Our friendship as far as it goes is real and strong," she noted. She told him about her father's death, putting more into words than she had with anyone, moved by the mood of the visit and the beauty of the valley. Back at Hazen's home, they awaited the return of James, "the Immortal" who had spent the day in Amherst. Ida had James's attention for a moment but was "too fluttering to hold him." She told herself she had gotten her lesson and her uplift and mustn't be greedy for more. Still, she was in a "funk of soul" because it was the "end of HJ" for her. He asked if she was going home. She said no, she was off to Boston. She fancied he looked disappointed. When she confided that telling the often cruel truth about Rockefeller had been a distasteful chore, James retorted, "Cheer up. If there's anything you should cherish, it's your contempts. Cherish your contempt, young woman[,] and strength to your elbow!" She quoted this remark to the end of her life. The searing Rockefeller sketch appeared a few months afterward; perhaps she put James's advice to use immediately.

She had a last glimpse of James as he departed, in the "noise, heat and confusion of the train — an indecent milieu for him and he was oppressed by it." She noticed his soiled cuffs and a smear of morning egg near his sensitive mouth. Even when in a state of rapture, Ida reported the whole truth as she saw it.

CHAPTER FIFTEEN

The American Magazine

IN NOVEMBER 1905, Sam sent Ida a secret prospectus for a major expansion of the McClure enterprise. She was not to tell Phillips about it. There had been earlier hints, both about Sam's plans and about Phillips's exclusion from them. A few years before, Sam had told her, "My dear dear friend, . . . I feel that after all, personally, you are the most important to me as an associate. I really feel that you hold the first place. I look forward to the time when you and I and Boyden and Baker will start our new magazine." Sam had previously confided to Ida that Phillips was too tired and she should take over some of his duties. She replied tartly that Phillips was "better than ever and that would not be a good use of [her] time." Now Sam was excluding Phillips altogether, undoubtedly because he foresaw his partner's disapproval.

The scheme that would finally drive Sam's writers and friends away forever included a new *Universal Magazine,* 1,000 acres of land for a model settlement, a people's university with curriculum and textbooks, a life insurance company, a universal library, and even a people's bank.

Ida knew that Sam wasn't motivated by greed; he had always simply wanted to run the world's most interesting magazine — and with it, correct all the world's abuses. In the midst of the crusade against trusts, Sam imagined he could create an empire of benevolent businesses, which to others sounded awfully like a trust. He was quietly seeking financial backing from railroad, banking, and insurance magnates.

Ida, Phillips, Boyden, and Steffens closed ranks to stop the scheme. The newly launched profession of public relations was using propaganda published as news to burnish the images of such entities as Standard Oil and such persons as John D. Rockefeller. Ida and her colleagues saw that Sam's new financial backers could easily make the magazine a public relations tool to promote their own interests. Determined to preserve the reputation of *McClure's,* Phillips and Ida demanded that the magazine be reorganized along democratic lines. Its mission had become too important to be managed by one man, and that man in particular.

In March 1906, Ida was on a holiday in Arizona with the Phillipses. She wired Bert that when they returned to New York, everything could be fixed. But if not, she added ominously, "we *can* secede."

Phillips, who had been feeling too old to change his life course, abruptly made up his mind when he got back. He would leave the magazine unless they persuaded Sam to turn it over to them. Ida agreed that she would too. They gave Sam an ultimatum in the spring of 1906: he must sign over a majority portion of his stock to be placed in trust, with the voting rights given to the four of them. It meant surrendering control of *McClure's.* Outside this meeting, Siddall, now on the staff, Steffens, and Boyden paced the hallway, awaiting word of their fate.

Sam signed the paper. Then he begged to be reinstated. He cried that he would rather sell his interests than lose control of the company. Ida reacted coolly and instantly, scrawling a new agreement that gave the dissidents an option to acquire all of Sam's stock at $1,000 per share. Phillips, his leg jerking nervously under the table, let her take charge. She pushed the new paper toward Sam. He signed and then fled in tears.

Within hours he had changed his mind again. Ida went to see him alone. "He referred to his love for me. . . . I feel he is not wholly sincere yet he thinks he is. . . . I ache dreadfully," she reflected in her journal. "At end, [Sam] sprang up and flung his arms around me and kissed me — left weeping I sit down and sob hysterically but am more convinced than ever that we are right."

Sam McClure at a worried moment.

The outside directors of the McClure Company decided to stick with their chief, as he was the "spark-plug of the editorial department." Sam wrestled with himself and won. "I cannot leave the magazine. I *simply cannot*," he wrote Ida. He had to put his own stock up for sale. He needed desperately to raise some cash to buy out his former colleagues.

So Sam McClure remained sole head and heart of the magazine he'd founded, hobbled with a massive debt. Ida and Phillips departed, taking Siddall, Baker, and Steffens with them. Baker and Steffens turned down offers of high salaries from competitors to stay with their comrades. According to the agreement negotiated with Sam, he was to pay each of them $3,000 a month for four months and $5,000 a month for thirty-five months to acquire their stock, and they had to complete the pending articles he had commissioned from them. Ida's last piece for Sam, published in March 1906, was titled "Commercial Machiavellianism." Using *The Prince,* Niccolò Machiavelli's sixteenth-century treatise on political realism, as her model, she described the ruthless pursuit of wealth for its own sake using force, craft, and treachery, arguing again that greed and deception were threatening American traditions. "Truth, nothing but the truth — ugly and cruel and relentless as it may be — is the cure for commercial Machiavellianism," she declared. A clause in the agreement allowed the departing staff members to start a new magazine.

In her autobiography, Ida called the group "derelicts without a job" who wandered into nearby Madison Square Park to sit on a bench and chew over their prospects. Only six months later, the "derelicts" produced the first issue of their magazine.

Later that year, Ida gave a lecture to Barnard College students called "Ethical and Intellectual Effects of the Modern Trust." The young women, in caps and gowns, listened raptly, according to the *New York Times*. Ida sarcastically compared the "human vultures" who ran the trusts to pirates who had lost their sense of humor, giving as an example an insurance executive who claimed his company was "benevolent," failing to see the "joke." Her audience understood her assumption that by design, companies could not be benevolent, since they took in money from customers to hedge against disasters. Abandoning her long-held belief that revolutions were not effectual mechanisms for reform, she predicted that sooner or later a revolution would restore ethics to business.

Ida, Phillips, Baker, Siddall, Steffens, and Boyden formed the Phillips Publishing Company. To raise the money to buy the *American Magazine,* formerly *Leslie's Monthly,* from its current proprietor, all of the principals lobbied their business and political connections. Armed with a prospectus promising dedication to reform and "joyous reading," they succeeded in collecting the necessary funds. The first issue was assembled at breakneck speed and appeared in October 1906.

Everyone had taken a pay cut. Ida's salary went from $8,000 per year at *McClure's* to $5,000. There would be exciting journalism again, even an office filled with many of the same brilliant colleagues. Bert Boyden was "the ringmaster of the whole show." But there would be no more Sam McClure, and she had loved him. "Was there ever so much fun in work? Or ever so much anguish of spirit when the thing exploded?" she asked a friend near the end of her life.

In March 1906, while Sam was embroiled in the collapse of his life's work, President Roosevelt had sent him a complaint, objecting to the tone and content of the magazine's articles: "It is unfortunate to encourage people to believe all crimes are connected with Business and that the crime of graft is the only crime." He asked that Steffens, in particular, "put more sky in his landscapes," meaning more emphasis on the positive, to add perspective. Sam was too preoccupied to pay attention.

McClure's was not the only magazine exposing corruption. The last straw for the president had been an article in *Cosmopolitan* called "The Treason of the Senate," which had appeared in February 1906. The charge that Congress could be bought and sold by plutocrats threatened the effectiveness of his administration.

Speaking off the record at a private dinner on March 17, 1906, Roosevelt stepped up his retaliation against investigating journalists. He compared them to the man with the muckrake in John Bunyan's *Pilgrim's Progress*, who kept his eyes on the mire rather than on the celestial crown. "There are beautiful things above and around them," Roosevelt said of certain unnamed journalists, "and if they gradually grow to feel that the whole world is nothing but muck, their power of usefulness is gone. If the whole picture is painted black there remains no hue whereby to single out the rascals for distinction from their fellows."

Word of this speech spread quickly, and Roosevelt decided to repeat it when laying the cornerstone for the House Office Building a few weeks later. Investigative journalists who had published in *McClure's* and other magazines assumed they were the president's targets. Privately, Roosevelt told Ray Baker that he was referring specifically to the Hearst-owned newspapers. But to others he accused "muckrakers" of promoting socialism, even revolution.

Roosevelt was biting the hand that fed him. Investigative journalism, by pointing out what needed fixing, had laid the groundwork for the positive domestic accomplishments of his presidency. Ida was stung by his attack and never really let it go. She wrote later, "I had hoped that the book [*The History of the Standard Oil Company*] might be received as a legitimate historical study, but to my chagrin I found myself included in a new school, that of the muckrakers." She pointed out that Roosevelt had misread Bunyan, whose pilgrim was raking riches, not mire. More than once, Roosevelt had referred to the tycoons of the day as "malefactors of great wealth." His meaning would have been clear, she said, had he referred to "muckrakers of great wealth" and called the reporters "malefactors." On one occasion, she challenged Roosevelt to his face, pointing out that she and Steffens were not stirring up "revolt" but digging up "facts." He retorted that they weren't "practical," meaning that they disregarded the realities of politics.

Theodore Roosevelt was the first president since Andrew Jackson to make the federal government an agent of social welfare. He claimed new powers for the presidency, justifying his increased authority by asserting that the power to do good now outweighed the power to do ill, should the "wrong kind of man" be elected. His friend the reformer Jacob Riis and the muckrakers had demonstrated that publicity spurred action. During his administration the Department of Commerce and Labor and the National Conservation Commission were created; a railroad rebate act, the Pure Food and Drug Act, an eight-hour workweek for women, and the National Monuments Act all passed.

An American aristocrat by birth, Roosevelt heartily disapproved of the robber barons. "I do not admire as a type the American money-maker, [or the] worse than recklessness of the Rockefellers, Harrimans and the like," he wrote a friend. The more he saw of the new filthy rich, the more profoundly he was "convinced of their entire unfitness to govern the country." He said he put his faith in the sort of common man who had supported Lincoln.

In 1907, the *New York Times* published the findings of an economist who claimed that 1 percent of Americans now controlled 90 percent of the nation's

President Theodore Roosevelt.

wealth. Fifty years earlier, wealth had been much more evenly distributed. Then, there had been only 50 millionaires. Now there were 800,000. The economist concluded that socialism, or an equal distribution of the nation's wealth, was the only answer to this grievous and unjust situation. Other economists disputed the figures, saying that the top 1 percent had only 20 percent of the wealth. In any event, they insisted, socialism was certainly *not* the answer to America's problem.

Many in the press assumed that President Roosevelt's muckraker speech had caused the breakup of *McClure's*. A rumor circulated that under pressure from the White House, Sam had ordered his staff to cease muckraking, whereupon the muckrakers had decamped, but it wasn't true.

For several years after the breakup, Ida's lawyer battled for rights and royalties owed her by McClure. "It is quite characteristic, I think, of the McClures to regard a contract as an instrument by which someone else is bound, but which they are at liberty to disregard," remarked the attorney. When he suggested that she sue, Ida refused.

CHAPTER SIXTEEN

Materfamilias

AFTER FRANKLIN TARBELL'S death in 1905, Ida took on responsibilities she'd avoided while he was alive. Her sister, Sarah, had given up painting in Europe to help nurse their father, then stayed on with Esther in Titusville. Will was carrying on the fight for Pure Oil's independence from Standard Oil. These apparent sacrifices only added to the guilt Ida still harbored over having gone off to Paris. And now, hard earned as it was, she lived a far more privileged life than the rest of her family did.

During that eventful spring of 1906, Ida found time to put a down payment on an old forty-acre farm near Redding Ridge, Connecticut. Perhaps she intended to establish a base for the surviving Tarbells or to turn her income from royalties into something tangible. Ida's sudden impulse prompted Bert Boyden to remark affectionately that she couldn't be trusted, and he had to go see the property to make sure the decision wasn't a mistake. "Of course you are an idiot and of course you cannot be cured," he told her. The impulsive purchase must have surprised all her friends. While she urged homemaking on other women, the concept was purely theoretical in her own case. Domestic life had never interested her. Her New York apartments were places to work, not to play house in. But the idyll of her infancy on her grandmother's farm was not forgotten.

She and Boyden were enchanted by the pair of ancient trees in front of the house and the babbling brook behind it. He urged her to buy the place and then took a proprietary interest in tastefully fixing it up. She called it Twin Oaks, which was also the name of the imposing Gardiner Hubbard home

Ida's farm in Connecticut.

where she had stayed in Washington — probably as a joke, as was naming the horse she acquired Minerva.

Once furnished, painted, and wallpapered, the farm still demanded upkeep; in fact, it seemed to devour money. Ida set aside a fund: one-third for house, one-third for land, and one-third for furniture. She began taking freelance writing assignments that weren't up to her usual standard just to earn enough to support the farm. She had the fields plowed and planted with corn and apple trees. Her caretaker, Paul Trup, got her to plant vegetables in addition to the flowers in the garden. She acquired a pig, chickens, Minerva the mare, and a cow she named Esther Ann, after her mother. The neighbors she befriended were unpretentious natives as well as the writers and publishers who were beginning to establish weekend retreats in the area. Mark Twain was building an eighteen-room villa not far away and invited Ida to luncheon there when it was completed.

Ida escaped to her farmhouse whenever she could and worked there at a big desk. Colleagues from New York came for uproarious weekend house parties. Ida was, as usual, the calm, approving center around whom spun the fun. After she got the hang of cooking with the built-in oven, Ida instituted an annual roast pig dinner for fifty neighbors and played the piano while they all sang.

Ida's city friendships were conducted in restaurants and clubs. While many men sought and enjoyed her company, her closest companions were other single professional women who were interested in public issues. A glimpse of one such gathering is provided by British novelist and former magazine editor Arnold Bennett. He jotted notes after lunching with Ida and her friends, Anne Morgan and Elizabeth Marbury, the first theatrical agent. The latter was "a very business-like woman. Fat. Human. Kindly. Shrewd. Very shrewd and downright in her remarks." Ida was "the most wistful and inviting of these 3 spinsters. A very nice kind face aged by hard work, by various sympathies, by human experiences. A soft appealing face, yet firm and wise. When asked to go down to Washington with Anne and Bessie [Marbury], she said, 'I've only just got back. I haven't been at my desk for four or five days.'" They were all "extremely interesting, all different, yet intimate, putting arms around necks and calling each other by Xtian names, coming together on a purely personal basis, just like men."

———— ✳ ————

Ida had become a national authority on business and ethics. Her journalistic triumph, achieved in the face of threats (such as her father's dire prediction, "They will ruin the magazine") but in the end without violence or loss, had given her a unique credibility and a great responsibility. Now she carefully weighed her next subject.

While she was still a young editor at the *Chautauquan,* she had listed the three great social wrongs in the United States: discrimination in transportation, such as Standard Oil's rebates, which hurt small businesses; tariffs, or taxes on imported goods, which raised prices for consumers; and private ownership of natural resources, which shifted wealth from the public to individuals. All three caused economic depressions and gross inequalities in wealth. Ida decided to write about the tariff. Unlike railroad rebates, tariffs were legal. She had to make the case that they were nevertheless very bad for the nation.

Early in 1906, she went to Washington to comb through the *Congressional Record* for testimony from the numerous hearings conducted on tariffs since the Civil War. She interviewed the people who had been involved in tariff legislation in recent decades, but got little out of them. Only former president Grover Cleveland, who had fought the tariff and was still actively opposed to protectionism, or high tariffs, wanted to help.

Her series in the *American*, beginning in December 1906, helped make the tariff one of the Progressive Era's major issues. She showed that protective tariffs favored big business and punished the consumer by raising prices for everyday goods. She witnessed and documented appalling working conditions, laborers' lack of home life, the misery of children warehoused until they were old enough to work (at fourteen). Woodrow Wilson, then president of Princeton University, lobbed her the usual patronizing compliment, saying she had written more good sense about the tariff than any

Ida, 1907.

man he knew. Nevertheless, in 1909, Congress passed the Payne-Aldrich Tariff Act, responding to cries for reform by defiantly raising the tariff to an all-time high. Reader interest in the series also rose. President Roosevelt, Ida noted, was unwilling to do the hard study needed to effectively oppose tariffs.

Ida included a searing portrait of Senator Nelson Aldrich, later a coarchitect of the 1909 Payne-Aldrich bill. In it, she laid bare crony capitalism's hold on government. Corporations, in other words, were already determining legislative outcomes. She wrote, "Mr. Aldrich's 'Protection' is hand in glove with every other Privilege — naturally it is for the same tribe [the rich]. . . . It is the friend of Wall Street, the enemy of Conservation . . . the opponent of . . . opportunity." Photographs of owners' mansions were interleaved with those of dismal workplaces.

The tariff series and the history of the Standard Oil Trust are Ida's greatest contributions to American historical writing on business. Both are passionate defenses of the hijacked American dream. Her clear, readable analyses made dry, complicated subjects not only accessible but also immediately relevant to the general public — those to whom that dream had been promised.

In the winter of 1907–8, Ida took a break from writing about the tariff to publish "Roosevelt vs. Rockefeller," describing the measures taken

This cartoon shows President Roosevelt as a hunter taking aim at several trusts.

NO LACK OF BIG GAME
The President Seems to Have Scared Up Quite a Bunch of Octopi.

to regulate monopoly since the publication of *The History of the Standard Oil Company.* President Roosevelt had gotten behind the effort to impose real punishments on runaway trusts. On November 15, 1906, the U.S. attorney general had filed suit against Standard Oil of New Jersey in a St. Louis court. The Department of Commerce and Labor, which Roosevelt had established to enforce laws governing business, sued Standard Oil over railroad rates and its monopoly of the oil business. The government won in 1909, a verdict that was upheld by the Supreme Court of the United States in 1911.

Ida also reviewed the company's recent actions in Kansas, showing that it continued to behave unethically. Her articles and the federal suits moved John D. Rockefeller to break his silence and publish in 1909 the coy autobiography *Random Reminiscences,* which offered a spare but sugarcoated account of his ascent and his justifications of Standard Oil's practices.

From time to time, Sam made plaintive appeals to Ida's affections. He said he was "starved for her," and dreamed she'd kissed him. Once he rang her city doorbell so late at night, she refused to see him. The dogged resolution with which Ida had renounced marriage, even love, at a tender age emerged again as a shield. Sam McClure, the incurable romantic, was tormented by the change in their relationship. It was clear that the parties to the *McClure's* "divorce" were bereft without each other.

Sam had lost his first-string players. Because he had had to buy them out, he was in effect paying them to publish a competing magazine, leaving him short of money as well as talent. The new owners of the *American* realized that without Sam's galvanizing drive, their work was wanting in passion. Ida alluded to this problem in a letter to young Bert Boyden, who had become her principal confidant: "We need a quality of effort . . . which we don't seem to have in the team. We always have lacked it. A certain hustle, ingenuity—a general energizing effect such as we used to get out of S.S. [McClure]. . . . It's a talent—a genius & we haven't it in the staff. . . . We have not *punched* hard enough editorially. . . . JSP [Phillips] sees it. He frets because he is not that kind and that [sic] nobody else is." Years later, reminiscing to Viola Roseboro', Ida wrote, "I think we had a good start on *The American.* . . . We missed the General, a certain radiance he gave to work. Though I think we always resented more or less what we felt he had done to us."

Lincoln Steffens wanted to make the *American* a socialist organ. Ida was withering in her rejection of that idea and of all ideologies. Resisting

The editorial staff of the American Magazine. *Seated, from left: John S. Phillips, Ida, Bert Boyden. Standing: Ray Baker (left) and John Siddall.*

A gathering at the farm, including Ida (with dogs) and Esther to her left.

partisanship, the magazine celebrated successful reforms rather than exposing ongoing corruption. For one such article, Ida went to Chicago in the summer of 1908 to report on the streetcar system after the city took it over from private owners, greatly improving service.

On her way back from Chicago, Ida stopped in Titusville. She found her mother ill enough to be checked in to a sanitarium. She took Sarah, who was also unwell, with her to Twin Oaks. Esther would spend most of her remaining summers in Connecticut, issuing instructions on managing the animals, the garden, and the house. Her mother's querulousness and self-pity took a toll on Ida's nerves, as they always had. Will was heard from regularly, needing to borrow money from his sister to pay mounting debts. He was no longer getting along at Pure Oil and quit within a few years.

CHAPTER SEVENTEEN

The Woman Question

THERE WAS NO subject that Ida cared more about than the nature of woman and her place in society. She thought of herself as an expert on the subject because she was a woman. And yet she was exceptional, as she was successful and at ease in a man's world. From the platform her success offered her, she warned other women to stay put. Ida changed her mind over time, but she stayed on the sidelines during the battle for suffrage, announcing that she opposed giving women the vote. When challenged, she marshaled inadequate intellectual arguments and murky emotional ones. Regrettably, they cloud her legacy. Despite the enormous significance of her work on Standard Oil and other matters, she disqualified herself as a fully positive example to succeeding generations of women.

While still an adolescent, Ida found the courage to reject her family's religious dogma and embrace Darwin's theory of evolution. A few years later, her study of Madame Roland convinced her that revolution led inevitably to violence. Assimilating these and other experiences, Ida became a gradualist, resisting sudden or rapid change, even for the better. And so, as the campaign for women's suffrage intensified in the early twentieth century, she naturally tried to slow it down.

Ida undertook to write as an authority about womanhood and women's role in society, although she had very little in common with most other women. Women had occupied a separate sphere from men for as long as she had been alive. They were considered a category of personhood, rather than human beings with the full rights of citizens. Most people, Ida among them, agreed that women possessed a special nature that differed from men's. She rejected the suffragist argument that women were "better than men and needed only the chance in politics to clear society of its corruption"; she believed women's value to society lay in their compassion and capacity for nurture. She feared that participation in the hurly-burly of electoral politics would corrupt those qualities, "vulgarizing" women. Suffrage could "undermine Woman's sense of individual responsibility, morals and manners."

Ida characterized the drive for suffrage as a misguided war on men. She acidly dismissed what she considered ignorant, intellectually dishonest campaigning for suffrage that "overemphasizes what they call the 'door mat theory,'" the claim that men walked all over women. She didn't sympathize with women who claimed to be victimized any more than she had with her mother's complaints or those she had heard as a teenager from women who had seemed to her no worse off than men. She tartly asserted that women's rights advocates overlooked "that you get new privileges in the world because it is necessary for the good not of yourself but of the whole." That suffrage was a human rights issue seemed not to occur to her, perhaps because, as an historian, she was much better at looking backward than she was at anticipating the future.

Her first major article on women's issues, "The American Woman," ran in the *American* from November 1909 to May 1910. She began by describing

In this cartoon ("Shall Women Vote?"), women in chains are denied the vote by venal politicians. Ida believed the opposite — that women voters would become dupes of party bosses.

the roles played by women in American history, from Revolutionary times through the Civil War, arguing, with the aid of many heroic examples, that wars had raised women's status and brought out their strengths in a world that was neither masculine nor feminine, but human.

She portrayed Abigail Adams, John Adams's wife, as a liberated woman, able to support the American cause without needing legal equality with men. According to Ida, Abigail Adams had felt equal in her heart; power and influence were inherent in her womanhood. Suspicious of privilege, Ida nonetheless ignored Abigail Adams's special position as future president John Adams's wife.

Ida didn't think she herself needed legal equality either. But she could hardly speak for the great majority of women, who didn't write for a magazine or have the ear of the president. In insisting that American women had served the nation well without the vote, Ida was defending a status quo that she thought preserved republican values of equality, fairness, and opportunity. The unchecked growth of industry and of cities threatened the traditional small-town existence she believed essential to the continuation of the American ideal. Women had the power to hold these forces at bay, if awakened to the danger. Describing, in reverential tones, the work of mothers and wives, she presumed to speak for those who rejected the noisy suffrage campaign being waged around them: "It is not bigotry or vanity or a petty notion of their own spheres which has kept the majority of women from lending themselves to the radical wing of the woman's movement. It is fear to destroy a greater thing which they possess. The fear of change is not an irrational thing."

While Ida opposed women's suffrage, she strongly supported women's liberation. In *The Business of Being a Woman,* published as a book in 1912, she paid tribute to "early disturbers of convention and peace" Elizabeth Cady Stanton, Susan B. Anthony, and their contemporaries:

> No woman who today takes it as a matter of course that she should study what she chooses, come and go as she will, support herself unquestioned by trade, profession or art, work in public or private, handle her own property, share her children on equal terms with her husband, receive a respectful attention on platform or before legislature, live freely in the world, should think with anything but reverence of these splendid early disturbers of convention and peace.

But she warned that the movement portrayed marriage as a trap, that unless she had a career, a woman would have to apologize for "never-having-done-anything!" Ida didn't pretend to be entirely objective about women.

That she had never married she blamed partly on her mother's unhappiness. And yet she warned younger women that her own success had been achieved at the sacrifice of her biological nature and its fulfillment. Girls had to understand the "essential barrenness of the achieving woman's triumph, its lack of the savor and tang of life, the multitude of makeshifts she must practice to recompense for the lack of the great adventure of natural living." A woman whose exclusive ambition was success in a business or profession had to defy her very nature and become cold. The result, though it might be "brilliant, [was] repellent."

She offered some slack to female misfits, presumably like herself:

> A few women in every country have always and probably always will find work and usefulness and happiness in exceptional tasks. They are sometimes women who are born with what we call "bachelor's souls" — an interesting and sometimes even charming, though always an incomplete, possession! More often they are women who by the bungling machinery of society have been cast aside. . . . But they are not the women upon whom society depends; they are not the ones who build the nation. The women who count are those who outnumber them a hundred to one — the women who are at the great business of founding and filling those natural social centers which we call homes. Humanity will rise or fall as that center is strong or weak. It is the human core.

In *The Ways of Woman,* published in 1915, she made specific the "fall" that would result from weak mothering: "To hold one man that he reverts neither into savagery nor sloth — one state or the other being his natural condition — is the greatest school on earth."

Did Ida feel scorned? Did she really regret her choices and consider her life barren? Did she think ordinary women lacked the spine to do what she had done? She clearly shared the common view that imitating men was a grave mistake. She was customarily described in the press as feminine in appearance and manner. In a way, it was a protective disguise. There was no denying that men and women were different. If the few women who did make it in the man's world, as Ida had, encouraged other women to do the same, she believed it would only unbalance sexual relations and bring misery to all.

Women could be hurt by the campaign for suffrage in other ways too. Electoral politics was, as she charged, often corrupt. Political parties could buy, bribe, or otherwise manipulate disempowered groups, such as immigrants, who would then vote as directed. Ida feared that women would either vote as their husbands did or become tools of party bosses. Such an outcome would only reinforce the idea that women didn't deserve the vote.

Accused by a prominent suffragist of betraying women, Ida wrote in a letter to Florence Kelley, a notable social and political reformer, that the suffrage campaign was too often imitating men. "I have done it myself. . . . I don't believe you know how hard it is really for me to feel that I am not altogether with you and Jane Addams, and a lot of other women, every one of whom is worth vastly more to society than I am."

Her sense of having been banished by her sisters was underscored when thirty-two-year-old Helen Keller, who had overcome deafness and blindness to achieve widespread admiration, expressed her shock over Ida's views. Keller declared Ida too old, at fifty-five, to comprehend the changing times. Stung, Ida related the remark to her friend Phillips. But he, too, was confounded by her opposition to women's suffrage, especially since he and

Ida agreed about nearly everything else. He accused her of being illiberal, contradictory, and vain, having a disappointing mind and character, and being too stubborn to admit she was wrong.

Ida didn't trust herself to respond in person and instead sent him a fourteen-page letter. She began by admitting that there might be some truth in what he said. "I have always found it difficult to explain myself, even to myself, and I do not often try." She felt she owed him an effort, even though "there is in feminine nature a strange barrier against complete self-revelation." So incisive about many subjects, Ida faltered when it came to matters whose emotional dimensions lay outside her own experience. With suffrage, she couldn't explain herself. Similarly, when Margaret Sanger, the crusader for birth control, asked Ida to lend her name to the campaign, Ida refused, claiming she didn't know enough about the subject, that "foggy intuitions . . . hold me back from what would be the easy way for me and that is to go along with you and the superior women in the movement." Elsewhere, she warned that women were too prone to "self discussion," which was "a serious handicap to both happiness and efficiency."

To Phillips, she quoted another woman's deprecating remark: "The only reason I am glad that I am a woman is that I will not have to marry one." Ida claimed to be a special case. Growing up with the suffrage movement, she had believed in it as much as in abolitionism and the protective tariff. Those who demanded the vote now behaved as if they were the first to have thought of it. She claimed to have taken the right to vote for granted, much as she had the right to a college education to fit herself for a man's work — "that was to be my contribution to the cause!"

She was not against suffrage, Ida continued; she was indifferent to it. She sympathized with women who wanted the ballot, but she saw it as the least important of their tools. The work she and Phillips had done in their magazines had shown that poverty, war, and ignorance could be defeated by education, but not by legislation. "You will gather from this that the chief reason I am not interested in the extension of suffrage is because I feel that it is part of what seems to me the most dangerous fallacy of our times — and that is that we can be saved morally, economically, socially, by laws and systems." Constrained by laws, she worried, people would lose their moral sense as one would lose unused muscle.

Years later, she told an audience at Allegheny College that her generation had helped erode standards of civility by overemphasizing careers and personal development for women. These individualist goals were antisocial; community was what nurtured democracy and equality. Ida's ideal society ran on goodwill, ethics, and natural law. Behavior could not be legislated, but must be implanted and nurtured — by women in their homes.

When Jane Addams learned, around 1910, of Ida's rejection of the suffrage movement, she observed, "There is some limitation to Ida Tarbell's mind." That hurt! But Ida told Phillips it was worth being "twitted" by her sisters, even publicly, "to be [proven] so sure and proud of women's value in the world — without the ballot." She did allow that the suffrage movement inspired some women to "help." "Let us be glad of every agitation that extends the sense of social obligation," she concluded.

Over the years, Ida continued to stress the importance of social obligation, by which she meant volunteer work. Despite criticism from activist women, she felt compelled (or stubbornly determined) to argue for private charity rather than government assistance for those who needed help, such as children, prostitutes, and unmarried pregnant women.

She could be counted on for conservative and candid opinions and became a default spokesperson for her sex. She frequently reiterated her belief that women's equality needed no proof and no legislation. She wrote

Jane Addams.

about the growing phenomenon of divorce, noting that the high number of divorces did "not appall," given the difficulties of marriage. "Women are casting off old forms of restraint — but no more than men. The human heart does not change." She was an advocate for female education at liberal arts, not vocational, schools, so that young women's minds would be opened. But they must also be equipped to work at permanent, not temporary, jobs. She observed that women were paid less than men because they worked an average of only three years before marrying and leaving the work force. Such women should not be left with nothing to do after their children were grown.

In "The Irresponsible Woman and the Friendless Child" in the May 1912 issue of the *American,* Ida called upon "unproductive . . . parasitical" middle-class women to go to the aid of homeless and neglected children. Idle wives were sending younger women the unfortunate message that "happiness lies in irresponsible living." As men were obliged to take part in public life, so women had an obligation to correct ills that afflicted the domestic sphere. Agencies and institutions alone could not do it. Well-heeled matrons should do more to spare poor girls from prostitution, principally by properly training their household help. (Ida's own record in this regard wasn't very good: three of her maids had to be dismissed for drunkenness, kitchen assignations, and, in one case, a self-administered abortion.) For Ida, society was a vessel: Its contents just had to be shifted around — a surplus of idle women here matched with a surplus of children there. It did not have to be emptied and refilled.

By 1924, when she published "Is Woman Suffrage a Failure?" in *Good*

Ida in her garden, around 1913.

Housekeeping, Ida had fully accepted suffrage, which had become law in 1920. She was ready to dispel the "myth of its failure," which only discouraged women from voting. Skeptical commentators had observed that women were slow to take advantage of the ballot and often voted in tandem with their husbands. But twenty million women did vote and should vote, she wrote. The notion that suffrage had failed was the same delusion that had led women to predict that suffrage would cure all ills. Women were now working in every area that men were. In her travels around the nation, she found that women were talking about politics and government, engaging in public affairs as never before. And Ida boasted that she knew half a dozen women who would be as able a president as any "since Lincoln."

Assessing suffrage again in 1930, Ida repeated that she had always believed that women could do more good for the world without the vote. She had expected that with the vote they would be tools of party bosses — just as men were — and that was what had happened. Her prediction that women would not exercise their new right in great numbers or run for office until another fifty years had passed was borne out. Not until 1980 did women outnumber men at the polls, as they do in the population, followed by a marked increase in the number of female candidates for office.

Over the years, Ida campaigned vigorously on behalf of women who had no choice but to work, often under horrifying conditions. In researching her tariff articles, she spent weeks witnessing the harsh reality in Rhode Island factories, where women labored for twelve-hour days. At the Triangle Shirtwaist factory in New York City, scene of a groundbreaking strike in support of union organizers in 1910, a fire resulted in the deaths of more than one hundred women who had been locked in their workspace and had hurled themselves from windows too high for engine ladders to reach. In the aftermath, Ida's workplace articles stressed safety measures and gave credit to businesses that had put them in place. "Death and mutilation are no longer considered the will of the Lord," she dryly noted.

Safety was linked to efficiency and to conservation, and all three were linked to increased industrial production. At the height of the Progressive Era, policymakers and intellectuals began looking to science, rather than legislation, to solve problems. Thus, the phenomenon known as Taylorism took managers of factories and intellectuals alike by storm. Ida came to believe that this system could improve women's work experience both in the factory and at home.

In the 1890s, Frederick W. Taylor began to break production down into small increments that could be performed by unskilled workers who would be paid piecework wages, thus cutting manufacturing costs while boosting production. Under the old, infor-mal system, workers could "soldier," turning out less than they were capable of doing, for fear that overproduction would cost them their jobs. Taylor, formerly a metal cutter, was convinced that workers were capable of producing more.

Frederick Taylor.

Under Taylor's system, workers performed their simplified, repetitious tasks while separated from one another, discouraging solidarity in the work force. Knowledge, authority, and skills were shifted from workers to management and the individual mechanic's initiative and

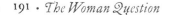

craft were sacrificed. The great mass of unskilled and often illiterate immigrant laborers could be easily integrated into the production line. Taylor argued that workers would internalize their managers' points of view and come to share an interest in the outcome of production. Taylor's disciples also asserted that the positive attitudes resulting from scientific management would shape good citizens — or, at any rate, docile ones.

Taylorism transformed the way Americans worked. Its principles were adopted not just in industry, but in school systems and the military, and they fostered the discipline of home economics. Ever on the lookout for ways to bolster domestic life, Ida recommended that Taylor's methods be applied to housework, making it more interesting — at least, to her — and thus an inducement to women to stay home. Ida believed that lack of respect for "the natural task," housework, made women uneasy, and that the solution was "to dignify, make scientific, professionalize that task." Soon, domestic science, or home economics, would codify and streamline the customs and skills that for generations had been passed from mother to daughter.

Taylorism changed the way Ida portrayed big business. In "The Golden Rule in Business," published in 1914–15, she described how managers could oversee progressive and humane shops. She visited more than fifty-five businesses to see how scientific management and Christian values worked together and concluded that scientific management was beneficial to everyone, the best way to protect workers and maximize profits. "Taylor believed, like Henry Ford, that the world could take all we could make, that the power of consumption was limitless," she wrote, with apparent approval.

Ida was a longtime member of the Taylor Society, as were other forward-thinking opinion makers. Taylorism's policies were consistent with her conservatism: they were derived from factual analysis that saved time and resources, discouraged workers from radical thinking, and encouraged rational, "Golden Rule" management.

All her life, Ida decried "unfairness," yet she was blind to society's unfairness to women. Perhaps the sacrifices she admitted to having made in order to succeed in a man's world caused a measure of self-loathing. In any case, while she insisted that women didn't need more "rights," she couldn't resist scolding them for not appreciating their natural gifts and for a frivolous preoccupation with clothes.

CHAPTER EIGHTEEN

Famous

AFTER TAKING ON new partners in a desperate attempt to keep it going, Sam McClure finally lost control of his magazine in 1911. He'd been a great editor but a lousy businessman. The magazine limped on for three more years without Sam, who took a job at the *New York Evening Mail.*

McClure had set out to publish the most exciting and accurate magazine around. For a few years, *McClure's* was at the top of the heap, shaping public opinion and policy. Ida was often mentioned in the press, not as a journalist or a reporter, but as a more highly esteemed historian and writer. By the time she was fifty, she was regarded with near reverence around the nation. McClure had made it happen.

The *American Magazine* under Ida, Phillips, and their partners was more interested in fair play than in muckraking, as Ida herself observed. Articles on popular culture predominated. In 1911, the partners decided to sell their operation to the Crowell Publishing Company, while supposedly retaining editorial control. The move

John D. Rockefeller Sr. with his bicycle.

worried Ida. She can't have been pleased when the *American,* under Crowell ownership, published "An Intimate View of JDR," featuring Rockefeller's dismissive remark that "Miss Tarbell's exposé was just commercialism. . . . Not one word [more] about that misguided woman." Rockefeller's fortune had recently passed the billion-dollar mark at a time when the median family income of Americans was eight hundred dollars, a ratio of 1,250,000 to 1.

Ray Stannard Baker reacted angrily when Crowell editors softened his left-leaning articles. Ida begged him to let it go. "I cannot bear the idea of another break-up. We shall be able to do far less if we are scattered. After all, it isn't much worse than some of the interferences of SS McC. . . . If they had refused to publish your article I should have walked out and I think the rest would, *but* the article is in," she wrote to him.

Ida was growing older, and buying the *American* had put her under financial strain. She was beginning to show signs of wear. She spent time at Clifton Springs to treat a sore arm; then, in California for several weeks, having agreed to participate in a seminar at Stanford, she succumbed to a fit of stage fright and cowered in her room rather than address a peace rally. She also "waffled" when coming face-to-face with the force of Theodore Roosevelt's personality in a chance encounter, even though she thought he was less amazing than he had been a few years before. Most telling of all, she urged her fellow editors to avoid controversy so as not to offend readers.

After declining to run for reelection in 1908, Roosevelt was staging a comeback for 1912. The Republicans renominated Taft. Roosevelt set out to rally the Progressives to a third party, called the Progressive ("Bull Moose") Party. Ida wasn't persuaded to lend her support, but on a visit to Titusville she found her fellow citizens longing for forceful leadership. She wrote Boyden that it was pathetic, how much people wanted to believe in somebody. She hadn't the heart to voice her doubts about Roosevelt to them. Still, when Ray Baker included criticism of Roosevelt in an article about the Progressives, she implored, "Give Teddy another chance. It will be a long time before people believe in a man as good." In late summer she wrote Boyden from Paris that the rich and connected expats expected Roosevelt to win the election. "The progressives are having the times of their lives getting drunk on visions of a world where there is no more 'environment of poverty.' Little things like campaign contributions and the tariff are too unimportant to be bothered about."

Ida voted for the scholarly, idealistic Woodrow Wilson, a Democrat, who won the election of 1912 in a landslide; Roosevelt came in a distant second. During the Roosevelt administration, big business had supported reforms as a way to protect the capitalist system from the socialist threat. Wilson's policies were a continuation of gradual change.

Ida spent the next few years writing as a workaday expert on business and labor conditions. "I never saw a machine I did not want to run," she

An imposing portrait of Ida, around 1915.

remarked one day, jauntily leaving a factory. Her delight in mastering mechanics and technology, both literally and on paper, made her a personality the public wanted to follow. Here was a woman unafraid to tackle masculine subjects while never appearing to be less than a lady. When she found enlightened owners and workplaces, she was glowing in her praise. Her critics, especially those who had cheered her attack on Rockefeller, were convinced that she'd gone soft. She retorted that readers applauded when she wrote about workers chopped up by machinery, and that when she wrote about factories where no workers were mangled, she was accused of selling out.

The incorruptible seriousness of purpose that characterized Ida at work was leavened by her zest for adventure. In 1913, at the age of fifty-six, outfitted in the aviator gear of the day, she went up in a seaplane, or "flying boat," and described the experience in an article, "Flying — A Dream Come True!" "I wanted to laugh and shout — the sense of exhilaration is one I have never known before," she crowed. High above the earth, she felt herself "a part of the whole thing." She waved gaily to a man in a boat far below and was tickled to see him wave back. The pilot suddenly swooped down to land on pontoons in the water. Men waiting on the dock wanted to see if she was shaking. Triumphantly, she held up two steady hands.

Ida had been a founder of the Authors' League, a collective that looked after the interests of writers. In 1914, to benefit the organization, the league proposed to some authors that they pick a scene from their work to be filmed for a motion picture. Ida went out to the Vitagraph Studios in Brooklyn, impatient with herself for agreeing to the project because it meant having to watch herself onscreen. But she found the collaborative aspects of the moviemaking process fascinating. Seeing all concerned contribute parts to the whole, she realized she had better perform hers as well as she could. She felt foolish pretending to write her piece on Lincoln under the eye of the camera, but respect for the professionalism of everyone involved out-weighed her self-consciousness. She told a reporter, "The only emotions I have to record are the haughtiness with which I went in and the meekness with which I came out." The woman who was regularly asked for her opinion on every important current issue could nearly always wryly poke fun at herself.

She moved to an apartment near the National Arts Club, where she could conveniently take guests for dinner. The sumptuously decorated club, with an art nouveau grand staircase, a pressed glass ceiling, parlors, and salons, admitted women from the start, unlike most other clubs for artists and literary figures. Ida belonged to a number of women's clubs as well, usually because she was invited to join. Such clubs promoted networking, which Ida believed American women badly needed — presumably because most were, as she had recommended, isolated in their homes.

In early 1914 workers at a Rockefeller-owned mine in Ludlow, New Mexico, had called a strike to protest miserable working conditions, low wages, and an order meant to prevent unionizing. Strikers and their families set up tent colonies outside the mine. Members of the National Guard and Rockefeller goons harassed the strikers, then rained machine-gun fire on them and set the tents ablaze, killing men, women, and children.

In response to the disaster, the Federal Commission on Industrial Relations was formed. It held hearings around the country to probe relations between labor and management in several industries. Ida was called to testify. Workers' problems, she said, were being solved by scientific management (Taylorism), and the unions ought to get aboard that moving train. Asked if corporate powers opposed women's suffrage as a way of keeping women's wages down, she denied it, saying wages were low because women lacked experience. She had observed in her travels to factories and shops

A woman union worker under arrest for protesting John D. Rockefeller Jr.'s actions at the Ludlow mine.

"a growing desire to give the common man full justice." Although press accounts stressed the crisp, spirited way she parried hostile questions, this performance did nothing to improve Ida's standing with feminists and labor organizers.

In 1915, John Phillips sold his remaining interest in the *American* to the Crowell Company. Rather than stay on as mere employees, the original partners resigned. Phillips became a consultant. John Siddall was made editor. Ida was once again a freelance writer, with complete freedom to do as she liked, except that she had to pay all the expenses formerly covered by the company—postage, travel, telephone, and her secretary's wages. She also had to keep her family afloat. After Franklin died, Will Tarbell took over the family's finances. When Ida couldn't make the numbers add up and asked him to sort things out for her, he put her off. Ida and her sister, Sarah, gradually realized that Will's debts and poor investments had undermined the family's financial security.

It was increasingly clear that Will suffered from mental illness. To help rescue the family's finances, Sarah put down her paintbrushes once again and learned bookkeeping. Ida accepted an invitation from a lecture bureau to tour Ohio and Pennsylvania, giving talks based on articles she'd written called "The Golden Rule in Business." She was paid $2,500 for forty-nine lectures in forty-nine days. Friends told her the assignment was beneath her and threatened her health, but she felt she had to take it. Typically, she made preparations to do the best possible job. Having been struck mute by stage fright in the past, and anticipating that once she managed to speak she might not be loud enough to be heard, Ida took voice lessons at an acting academy.

Her lectures on the Chautauqua circuit were usually given in small halls and circus tents. Now Ida was deeply moved by the solemn faces of working people staring expectantly up at her. "All my pretty tales now seemed terribly flimsy. . . . They listened so intently to get something and the tragedy was that I had not more to give them," she wrote. She traveled six weeks at a time twice a year for two years, enduring the uncertainties and indignities of life on the road.

President Wilson asked her to serve

Ida, 1917.

on his tariff board, advising on trade policy, citing her superior common sense on the subject. She would be the first woman to accept such a post, and Jane Addams begged her to take it for the sake of all women. But she did not. She thought it would be futile; she was an observer, not a negotiator. Besides, she had to concentrate on her obligations — the many Tarbells who depended on her. Ever since she'd been in her teens, financial security had been her abiding concern. And now she regarded nieces, nephews, and even grandnieces and grandnephews as dependents.

In the spring of 1917, Wilson, having won reelection as the peace candidate, declared war on Germany, bringing America into World War I. The president wanted America to take the lead in peace negotiations, and it had to be a combatant to do so.

Ida did accept Wilson's nomination to the Women's Defense Committee, charged with overseeing women's contribution to the war effort. It was studded with suffragist members who were at first aghast at her appointment, but later came to appreciate her warmth and group spirit. The distinguished magazine the *Nation* praised her ability to analyze and interpret difficult technical subjects and remarked that while Ida's writing was marked by its "definiteness," in person she was quite moderate. "Her whole appearance speaks this. Of good height and slender but strong figure, with a face well balanced in features and thoroughly feminine in cast, eyes that are both sincere and pleasant in expression, and a nicely modulated voice, there is not about her the slightest suggestion of 'opinionation.' . . . A broad charity forbids her confusing men and things. Hers was the gift of being able to 'hate the sin and love the sinner.'"

Ida saw that the committee had been cleverly set up to defuse rivalries among women's groups around the country eager to help the war effort. The committee had to appeal to the all-male Council of National Defense for its marching orders, a procedure much resented by militant suffragists, and Ida was frequently the go-between. There was so much work to do that she canceled two book contracts. She was losing weight and suffering from stress. The crisis meant that everyone was overworked. This time she couldn't skip off to Clifton Springs for a rest cure.

The committee addressed such mundane matters as methods for preserving food but also tackled issues involving women in the labor force, now that so many men were fighting overseas. Women were replacing men in factories, usually with an understanding that they were necessary to the war effort and only temporary workers. What would happen to them when the war was over? Jane Addams had despairingly predicted that all their

The Women's Defense Committee. Ida is seated second from left.

hard-won progress in wages and working conditions would be lost. Ida disagreed. The committee envisioned a future federal agency for women, to protect new perceived rights. The militants would accept nothing short of a position in the president's cabinet, akin to secretary of state. The suffragists were picketing; women chained themselves to the White House fence, defiantly inviting arrest. Ida's lifelong disapproval and suspicion of privilege spiced her view of this stage of the suffrage battle. At the Colony Club, a women-only private socal club, she saw wealthy matrons step up their militancy and questioned their motivation. "You see I do not think they had ever realized before that there was something they hadn't got and being the kind of ladies who want everything and were accustomed to getting it, they went out tooth and nail after suffrage," she wrote, ignoring the fact that most anti-suffragists were wealthy women.

Ida gave herself a pat on the back for her own restraint, even claiming later that such patience was responsible for finally getting the Nineteenth Amendment, legalizing women's suffrage, passed in 1919.

Meanwhile, domestic reform and free speech were sacrificed to war mobilization. The Wilson administration's War Industries Board canceled the Sherman Antitrust Act. Eugene Debs, the Socialist candidate for president, was sentenced to ten years in prison for speaking against the war. Others were prosecuted for criticizing the Red Cross, the YMCA, and the national budget. Ida saw the effects of this when she lectured around the country: war fever on one hand, pacifists afraid to speak their minds on the other. She found herself again pondering the fate of the American dream amid senseless worldwide conflict. It seemed like a subject that had to be tackled in fiction.

But before she could begin, her mother died. Later that day, September 2, 1917, Ida attended a wedding without mentioning her mother's death to anyone; imposing her loss on a joyful occasion would have been unthinkable. Then she traveled to Titusville, where she arranged the funeral and put her childhood home up for sale. Exhausted, she struggled back to Washington and collapsed. She was rushed to Johns Hopkins Hospital, where doctors found a spot on her lung; it was tuberculosis. Before antibiotics, this was a life-threatening illness, though not as dire as it had been in the previous century, when almost all tuberculosis patients wasted away and died. Ida remained in the hospital for three months. Few people were informed. Bert Boyden knew, of course, and arranged daily delivery of flowers.

Ida experienced difficulty swallowing and a weak, trembling leg. Her doctor recognized Parkinson's disease, for which there was no treatment at all. Accordingly, he didn't tell her, but simply advised her to get on with her life. The tremor worsened over the years, and her handwriting eventually became illegible. Finally she shook too much even to hold a Dictaphone. In the meantime, she got on with her life.

Back in New York, she went to work on her novel. Called *The Rising of the Tide,* it tells of a small midwestern town between 1914 and 1918. The setting was inspired by Poland and Titusville and by the glimpses of everyday America that Ida's tours afforded her. The character most like herself is a strong-minded young schoolteacher married to a muckraking editor who is killed in the war. She described the book not as a novel but as a record of what small-town people thought and felt about the war. John Phillips came over often to give her editorial help. He never told her the book was a literary embarrassment, and he may not have thought it was. The *New York Times* reviewed it, beginning by tactfully commending Ida's self-sacrificing work on the Women's Defense Committee, then calling the book "almost amazingly lacking in both dramatic and narrative sense." Ida mentioned neither this failure nor her illness in her autobiography.

When the war ended in 1918, the victorious powers looked for ways to punish Germany and contain Russian Communism, redrawing boundaries in Europe and the Middle East. Wilson had a plan to ensure peace by rebuilding the economies that had been destroyed, but France and England were bent on revenge. They dismantled the Austro-Hungarian Empire and ordered Germany to pay reparations it couldn't afford. Ida angrily predicted that the peace terms guaranteed another war.

Many of the old *McClure's* crowd were in Paris during the Paris Peace Conference, where the terms were decided. Ray Stannard Baker was there as an assistant to President Wilson. John S. Phillips edited the *Red Cross Magazine,* headquartered there. Ida was unaware that Wilson had given her a spot in the official U.S. legation so that she'd have greater access to news than just a press pass would provide. Secretary of State Robert Lansing vetoed it, however; he would not have a female on his team. Ida wasn't told of this insult and as usual desired no special privileges anyway. Observing the peace process for the *Red Cross Magazine,* she found that hate was replacing idealism and went to bed one night weeping tears of despair.

The pleasure-loving Paris she had known in the nineties was no more. Her old friends there had all suffered without basic necessities during the war. She hauled cases of gifts for them from America, including a huge heavy ham that rolled off a train luggage rack onto luckless aid workers in their seats.

She had previously agreed to a Chautauqua speaking tour and in 1919 set out for the Northwest, sometimes sleeping in a tent, to spread her understanding of what had happened at the peace conference. An aggressive campaign was being waged against the League of Nations by conservative factions, but Ida's destinations were so remote and isolated, she felt that audiences there would make up their own minds. She was sickened when the league was defeated in Congress as President Wilson lay helpless in the White House after a stroke.

———— ✳ ————

As the Roaring Twenties began, Ida was sixty-three years old, attempting a dignified transition to useful old age while the fickle nation went gaga over

Flappers having fun near the Capitol.

youth, crime, stunts, and having a good time. Rebellion against bourgeois respectability spread rapidly as radio suddenly allowed the entire nation to experience every new fad simultaneously. The reasoned, conscientious journalism Ida practiced was being overshadowed by the modish debunking style of H. L. Mencken, a libertarian writer and editor of the *American Mercury.* He specialized in skewering the "booboisie" and social reformers, among many others, in an elegant, aphoristic style. Although Mencken, like Ida, championed scientific progress, he was a satirist whose targets were the very small-town virtues she held dear.

Ida had been terribly shaken by the war and the hysterical fear of Communism that rose in its wake. She said later she'd even lost her curiosity. "Human affairs seemed to me to be headed for collapse. . . . What I most feared was that we were raising our standard of living at the expense of our standard of character." She observed that local individuality was being smoothed over by a homogenizing culture in America. "Standardization is the surest way to destroy the initiative, to benumb the creative impulse . . . essential to the vitality and growth of democratic ideals." She saw no contradiction in her embrace of Taylorism.

Nevertheless, making a living and bearing witness to the world's problems were for Ida reasons to carry on. In 1921, for the still-extant McClure Syndicate, she covered the disarmament conference held in Washington. Britain, the United States, Japan, and France promised to respect one another's rights and those of China. Ida's articles were published as a book called *Peacemakers — Blessed and Otherwise.*

The former representative of a London publisher conceived the idea of charging authors a commission to represent them in dealings with publishers and pursued Ida as a client. For a time, she resisted his importuning, but he persisted, became her literary agent, and increased the fees she earned for her articles. "You will be the salvation of my old age!" she told him.

Warren Harding succeeded President Wilson, tilting government bias back toward big business. Popular, genial President Harding promised a return to what he called "normalcy," or freedom from the foreign influences to which Wilson had been subject. Harding's White House offered a haven to American business and good times to American citizens. Peacetime meant an explosive growth in consumer spending. The automobile and home heating with oil represented opportunities for independent oil producers to gain a share of the ever-expanding market in petroleum.

Ray Baker wrote Ida that after trying for years, the librarian at Amherst College hadn't been able to locate a copy of Ida's *History of the Standard Oil Company,* now out of print. He wondered if there had been underhanded ways of removing it entirely from circulation. Ida replied that she used to scoff at that idea but now wasn't so sure. Other librarians had made similar complaints. She told him she planned to republish the *History* with new material.

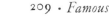

CHAPTER NINETEEN

Business Redeemed

*I*N 1924, WILL'S mental illness finally forced Ida to make a hard choice: she could either put him in an institution or install him and his wife, Ella, in her farmhouse. She chose the latter. She gave up her bedroom and the one next to it to Will and Ella and slept downstairs in a narrow room with one window, under a coverlet her mother had made out of old gowns formerly worn by Tarbell women. The change meant the end of carefree entertaining for Ida, but not for Will. According to a notice in the local newspaper, he built a fancy hen house and threw a stag party to inaugurate it.

Never willing to admit to feeling overburdened by Will, Ida claimed she found his cycles of mania and depression "interesting," even when he drew a gun on her and threatened to kill himself and Ella before, as he said, they froze to death. Sarah wasn't so tolerant. Will convinced himself that Sarah had embezzled money from Ida and then ordered her not to tell Ida that he thought so. Their older sister, he reminded Sarah, hadn't been exposed to the emotional storms that racked the Tarbell household after she left for college. This was an indication of long-simmering resentment that Ida was surely aware of and felt guilty about. He ordered Sarah to repay the money. Sarah told Ida what was going on, and she consulted a lawyer, admitting to him that Will had already become a kind of public nuisance in their neighborhood.

Ida considered getting a restraining order against her brother and tried to put him in the Wadsworth Sanitarium in South Norwalk. She persuaded Dr. A. D. Wadsworth himself to talk to Will and calm him down. She told the doctor that Will had been okay the previous summer, "keeping bachelor's hall" in her house and enjoying it, but that in the fall the mania had returned.

At a time when mental illness was barely whispered of, Ida was remarkably forthright in her communications with her lawyer and doctors. The attachment expressed in the old letters from his "lady love" to "my sweetheart" remained strong. Ida still thought Will was extraordinary — egotistical, impractical, improvident, irresponsible, charming. When he was calm, they enjoyed companionable times around the radio, occasionally hearing Ida referred to on the air.

If she confided in someone outside the family, it was probably Bert Boyden. In 1921, Bert wrote her that he had run into Sam McClure and Sam was "living proof of the fact that no one ever changes." Their former boss exuded the "same brilliance and pep but I was more impressed than I ever have been before with the different blanks that he has in his makeup." McClure kept bringing up "those people" who had done him in. He rattled off statistics just the way he used to — repeating some as often as twenty times in Boyden's presence. And he said he was starting a new magazine!

It wasn't really new. *McClure's* had gone bankrupt and been bought by a publisher who reinstated Sam in the editor's chair. It was Sam who proposed that Ida write a new chapter of *The History of the Standard Oil Company* for the magazine. She was feeling the pressure of passing years—how much time was left to her? The great work of her life had to be brought up to date and certainly restored to print. But no sooner had she written a few thousand words than *McClure's* folded again. The financial backer had forbidden Sam to publish a story on the Ku Klux Klan unless both sides were represented. "I personally know of some good things it has done," said Sam's sponsor. Sam ended their association.

The Appleton publishing company proposed that Ida write a biography of Judge Elbert H. Gary, chairman of the board of U.S. Steel, the first trust to be incorporated. To accept the assignment, she had to overcome her distaste for Gary. She wrote the Appleton editor: "As I look at him he is one of the best types that the 'hard-boiled' big business period has produced, but the best of that period does not stir me to great enthusiasm." Ida mentioned the Gary proposal to Sam; he, meanwhile, had found yet another new backer to prop up the magazine. This one was enthusiastic about a Gary biography, and Ida agreed to serialize it in *McClure's* first. She and Sam hoped it might attract enough readers to rescue the magazine yet again.

There was a fair chance that Gary's story would become a bestseller. Business and businessmen were hot topics during the Harding and Calvin Coolidge administrations. Where once ordinary Americans had saved their respect for the professions—law and medicine and teaching—they now identified their own interests with those of big companies. Everyone admired and wanted success. The growth of credit and installment buying fueled both wealth and spending. Suddenly, nearly every town had a Rotary Club, where businessmen found fellowship. People discovered that even the Bible provided useful guidance for making deals; books about Jesus as an exemplary businessman were popular. Muckraking was barely a memory. Its very success in reining in abuses had made it irrelevant.

U.S. Steel was run according to the Gary code, a paternalistic business ethic in harmony with the Golden Rule. In 1914–15 Ida had already published a series in the *American* titled "The Golden Rule in Business." She had visited a plant where nonunion immigrant employees had finally gone on strike to improve their wretched working conditions. Several were murdered by strikebreakers. In her article Ida asked if the tragedy could have been avoided had the plant been run like U.S. Steel, guided by the Golden Rule.

As someone who had run a giant corporation along ethical lines, Gary was a comparatively dry subject. Ida felt she understood him and his values. His forebears were New Englanders like hers and like Lincoln's. He had grown up in Illinois and become a lawyer and then, briefly, a judge, before he was appointed head of U.S. Steel. Gary and the labor union were at odds, but the company had instituted profit sharing, safety measures, and other workers' benefits. Some critics saw profit sharing as a way of pressuring workers to buy up watered, or excess, stock and give them the illusion of partnership in the corporation, while forbidding them to organize and keeping wages low. But Ida found Gary to be a model of rectitude. As Rockefeller had invented the bad trust, Gary was the architect of the good one.

Ida expected to be accused of whitewashing if she failed to denounce Gary. When her cautiously admiring biography came out in 1925, she was widely scorned for having been "tamed" by Gary. The series was reviewed in the *Nation* under the title "St. Elbert and the Heavenly Trust." The reviewer charged that Ida's work on Standard Oil had "developed in her a sort of suppressed desire for a 'fairy trust'" — in other words, a benign one. Ida may have been stung, but she didn't show it. The predators in business had already been thoroughly exposed, she observed in her own defense. There was another side to the story, and she had told it honestly. Gary was the heir not of Rockefeller and his commercial Machiavellianism, but of old-time American enterprise and its Christian code.

Compared to the nineteenth-century trusts, U.S. Steel under Gary exhibited some social responsibility. Ida had argued for regulation of trusts and won: Gary ran U.S. Steel by the new rules. She had to approve of his management style. The new struggle against big business was waged by labor and unions. Ida was suspicious of unions, with a few exceptions, on the grounds that they were often as guilty as management of abusing their powers. As her enthusiasm for Taylorism indicates, she saw every issue from management's point of view. This attitude put her out of step with younger liberal commentators, who regarded the venerable puritan values she affirmed as hindrances to progress.

Ida endured two unexpected and painful losses in the 1920s: John Siddall died of cancer in 1923 at age forty-eight, and two years later her beloved Bert Boyden succumbed to pernicious anemia at fifty. He had told Idarem (the nickname had stuck) that her friendship meant more to him than anything in the world.

She had to carry on. Her Lincoln files were so full, she could always churn out a book about him when she needed funds. *In the Footsteps of the Lincolns,* published in 1924, "rescued" the Lincolns from the "ranks of poor white trash where political enemies had so loved to place them." By tracking records from New England, Ida proved that her pioneer hero's forebears had been respectable Anglo-Saxon Protestants in the Puritan — indeed, the Tarbell — tradition.

Ida and Sam had counted on her Gary series to ignite circulation at *McClure's;* instead, it rang the magazine's death knell. *McClure's* was quietly sold to William Randolph Hearst in 1925 and became *McClure's, the*

Sam (standing), Willa Cather, Ida, and writer Will Irwin in Madison Square Park, 1924.

Magazine of Romance. Those who had hailed its part in the creation of the muckraking era in 1903 must have wept.

The next year, *McCall's Magazine* sent Ida to Florida to write about the deflation of the real estate boom. This most frenzied of the land and building frenzies of the twenties had peaked in 1925, then dwindled after widespread defaults and two hurricanes. Ida was tempted to buy a few bargain acres, she told Phillips, adding that he was not to worry; she wouldn't follow through. Her Florida visit was only an interlude, but a significant one. *McCall's* liked what she wrote and decided to send her to Italy to discover the truth about dictator Benito Mussolini. Was he a benign force, turning

Italy into an efficient modern state, or a threat to world order? *McCall's* would pay $25,000 for four installments, a very large sum.

Since World War I, Italians had been impoverished, ill governed, and inflation ridden, the elite terrified by the idea of Communism. In confident, mesmerizing speeches that won over all segments of the population, rising political star Mussolini ("Il Duce") outlined a socialist vision incorporating capitalism. His ill-equipped army in mismatched black shirts had marched on Rome and taken over the tottering government without bloodshed in October 1922. Promising order and efficiency as leader of the National Fascist party, he was soon running a totalitarian state. His blocky visage glared from walls and lampposts, and his black-shirted goons threatened anyone who showed disrespect. Once his rule was secure in Italy, the rest of the world took him seriously. *McCall's* wanted its first piece in a hurry, before the story (which Ida titled "The Greatest Story in the World Today") grew cold.

Ida thought that the Fascist takeover of power was the most amazing transfer of government she knew of. She was otherwise ignorant of events in Italy, but expected that a close look at an economic system operated as a corporate state would be extremely enlightening. The State Department warned that she might be arrested on Italian soil; other Americans had been, usually for drinking too much and loudly attacking the regime. "We do the same thing here [arrest opponents] now and then, you know," said the U.S. official. But Ida was determined to go.

On her way to Italy she saw her old friend Jaccaci in Paris. He, too, cautioned that she'd be frisked and mustn't carry any material hostile to the government. She *was* taking such material with her, she told Jaccaci, and did not propose to give it up without a struggle. Told that the Fascist salute would be required of her, she practiced it before the mirror in her hotel room.

But these things did not come to pass. She stayed more than four months in Italy and wasn't bothered by anyone. She ran into critics of Mussolini, but most Italians considered him a better solution to their problems than anarchy had been. She was moved by the sight of men, and especially of women, at work. This was a people who, six years before, had lived in chaos and now enjoyed order. The diversity among Italy's various provinces made Ida regret the growing standardization at home, where formerly distinctive regions were imitating the trendsetting coasts.

After touring for four months, she was granted, with the help of the American ambassador, an interview with Mussolini. Afterward she referred, more than once, to Il Duce's dimpled smile. This was to expose her to ridicule. Sly Viola Roseboro' was vacationing in Italy at the time. Of Mussolini's effect on Ida she said, "Here was one of the males who in other days and circumstances would have filled young Ida's dreams for a while. . . . I heard her let go about that dimple several times. All those things that are at such a variance with the old work horse she calls herself and to the serious worker she is and is known for pleases me a lot."

Ida compared Mussolini to Napoleon. But probably she and Sam McClure, who had his own infatuation with Il Duce, imagined him as an unleashed Teddy Roosevelt, finishing the work of the Progressive Era at the small price of a few civil liberties. Mussolini had his own version of Taylorism and the power to fully enforce it.

Ida later lamented the "awful lawlessness in [suppressing] liberty and free speech" under Mussolini, adding that he was "Platonic"; he "got poets out of the state. Poets upset the machine. Someone had to do it." But Ida did not explicitly address Fascism's incongruity with democracy. She went to see Italy on its own terms and found its economy stabilized by "thrift, hard work, development of resources and . . . legitimate colonization in the parts of the earth where he [Mussolini] could obtain land, by treaty or by purchase."

Ida and Roseboro' visited Siena together. Ida told her friend ahead of time to reserve the best rooms, as *McCall's* would pay. Roseboro' apparently took charge of other arrangements as well, such as meals and touring. She reported to John Phillips: "IMT is a mighty poor hand at taking care of herself. She has the theory of doing it all right but the winds of temptation overcome her. I never expected to see myself bossing and lecturing her the way I am doing and all who love her owe me gratitude."

Ida's thinking was evolving in sometimes surprising ways. In 1928 she spoke to female undergraduates at Knox College. "Life isn't interesting to a woman who is idle," she told them. Such women were pitiful. It was women's duty to "do their part to adjust the inequalities of wealth which are so great. . . . I don't believe it is possible for the married couple of today to get what they want out of life unless the wife works." This was far in advance of most opinion as well as contrary to her own earlier statements.

Ida admired her friend Herbert Hoover, with whom she had worked on unemployment issues during the Harding years, but in 1928 she supported the Democrat Al Smith for president. An engineer/bureaucrat, not a politician, Hoover was more conservative than Ida was. She believed that Smith had mastered the applied science of government and would further the people's welfare. Smith also pledged to end Prohibition, which Ida thought was a foolish and pernicious law. When she said so publicly, she received an avalanche of indignant, sometimes loony letters and seems to have patiently replied to every one, explaining that she believed in obeying the law and that Prohibition invited people to flout it.

That same year, Ida was profiled in the *New York Herald Tribune* as "the possessor of a keen mind that any man would envy." The article continued, "Yet, Miss Ida Tarbell is, above all, a woman. One who loves her home so much she runs two of them." Presumably, Ida was gratified by this characterization. In the same article she was quoted as saying, "Women's equality is too obvious to need proof. Women should not compete; men must remain producers and protectors."

Hoover won the election. One of Ida's fears about a Republican administration was borne out when a new tariff, the Smoot-Hawley Act, was passed after the stock market crashed in October 1929. The tariff helped to spread the depression to Europe. Hoover believed that the tariff produced prosperity at home, but Ida had concluded that it benefited only the wealthy. "Centralized wealth breeds arrogance," she wrote.

After the crash, banks began to fail. A catastrophic drought in the Mississippi Valley in 1930 doomed the country to a prolonged depression, since the Hoover administration seemed to have no good remedies for either man-made or natural disasters.

In 1931 Ida began work on her third and last business biography, the life of entrepreneur and industrialist Owen D. Young. Like Judge Gary, Young came from solid Protestant stock. He grew up on a farm and then practiced law, later becoming president and chairman of General Electric. Under his leadership, the company manufactured ever more desirable electrical appliances, which, because they were consumer products, cushioned General Electric from the worst effects of the Great Depression. In 1919 he had founded the Radio Corporation of America at the request of the government, which wanted to prevent the takeover of American radio by foreign entities. Young then created the network called NBC.

He had advised every president since Wilson and chaired committees in

Europe that determined German reparations payments mandated by the Treaty of Versailles. In 1929, Young was *Time* magazine's Man of the Year. A poll of his peers voted him the best businessman in America, beating Henry Ford and Herbert Hoover.

Ida admitted she was composing a eulogy. Young's record of public service distinguished him from old-style profiteers, and she wanted to celebrate it. He was a steward both of business and of national life. Her book appeared in the midst of a groundswell of support for a Young presidential run. He wasn't a candidate, but some reviewers thought the book amounted to a campaign biography and therefore was not of interest to serious readers.

The economic crisis that had begun in 1929 grew steadily worse. Franklin Delano Roosevelt (FDR), Theodore Roosevelt's young cousin, won the 1932 presidential election and used radio to reach and unite the American people. In his inaugural address on March 4, 1933, while more banks failed, unemployment soared, and insurrection was in the air, FDR was unsparing in describing the dire situation. He called for a new morality, for an end to greed, and for a renewal of the social compact. A just society must take care of its neediest members, he insisted. In their editorials, some conservative newspapers, not as confident that the current government could save the nation, called for a dictatorship. Publisher William Randolph Hearst produced a movie called *Gabriel Over the White House,* depicting the president as a benevolent but totalitarian ruler. FDR was not even an ideologue holding fixed beliefs, and he certainly was not a dictator. Absolute rule had returned, however, to Germany, Italy, and Russia.

Ida had modest investments in the stock market. When the market crashed in 1929, she didn't panic, but her situation was far from secure; she helped support her nieces and nephews, their children, and eventually even their grandchildren. When historian Arthur Schlesinger Sr. had asked her in 1923 to contribute to a series he was editing called *A History of American Life,* she reluctantly agreed, fearing that sweeping academic history was not her forte. She had started researching *The Nationalizing of Business* but put it aside so often to write something more lucrative that she didn't deliver the manuscript to Schlesinger until 1936. According to the editor's introduction, her comprehensive account covered "the maldistribution of wealth, the paradox of poverty amidst plenty, the . . . business cycle . . . capital and labor . . . farmer . . . the danger to democratic society of vast economic power vested in irresponsible hands." Although Ida had worried that she wasn't qualified to write an academic history, it makes surprisingly lively reading and, like all her work, is thorough and accurate. Despite her efforts, however, money didn't come in as it had in the glory days at *McClure's.*

As she grew older and more vulnerable, Ida became increasingly susceptible to the attentions of an importunate heiress called Ada Pierce McCormick, who for years strove to establish a worshipful friendship with her. McCormick, who first met her in 1923, was decades younger than Ida and apparently saw her as a mother figure. Ida was a crusty mother, but she submitted to interviews and Ada recorded everything she said, hoping eventually to publish Ida's biography. Impatient with McCormick's

Ada McCormick.

requests for writing advice, Ida referred her to Viola Roseboro'. McCormick thereafter paid the indiscreet Roseboro' five dollars per letter for affectionate, but often catty, anecdotes and opinions about her former colleague.

Aware that Ida was in need, McCormick pressed a loan on her and then went behind her back to ask old friends to take up additional collections. This idea was indignantly rejected by everyone who knew how embarrassing it would be to Ida.

In 1931, McCormick, who lived in Tucson, arranged for Ida to lecture on biography at the University of Arizona. During her stay in Tucson, Ida fell sick and often lay helpless in the face of her hostess's intrusions and petty jealousy of others who had any claim on Ida's affections. One such person was Ida's friend Jane Addams, winner of the 1931 Nobel Peace Prize, who happened to be in Arizona and attended Ida's lectures. When McCormick suggested Addams come to lunch so they could all indulge in some girl talk, Ida snapped that she and Addams discussed important national issues together and said Addams would grab her hat and flee if McCormick tried to invade her privacy.

No matter how sharply she was rebuffed, McCormick was unrelenting in her effort to extract some show of warmth from Ida. McCormick compiled a large file with notes for a biography of Ida, but Ida never granted the affection she sought — only a rueful gratitude for McCormick's financial help. McCormick's loans ensured that she and Ida remained linked.

Ida was reserved with women friends who wanted more in the way of intimate disclosures and dependency than she could bestow. Ida and Roseboro' both corresponded with John Phillips as they grew old and distance prevented visits. Roseboro' wrote to Phillips, "[Ida] gives me little besides benevolence. . . . I know I have broadly speaking nothing to give her; not even as a first class listener." Such was Roseboro's frustration with Ida's distracted goodwill. But McCormick remarked that Ida "never spoke unkindly of anyone — except under the stimulus of Viola Roseboro's humorous and unsparing tongue."

When she was in New York, Ida worked in her studio near Gramercy Park. The long, narrow, high-ceilinged room was furnished with a pair of desks, the Dictaphone that McCormick had given her, several chairs, piles of newspapers, a sofa, bookcases, and files. Visitors opening one of her books might dislodge a flower put there to be pressed, but it's hard to imagine any visitor daring to do so. Though Ida's usual attire was plain black and her glasses hung on a black ribbon, people spoke of her luminous personality. She always looked aristocratic to them. Her posture, until Parkinson's destroyed her balance, was ramrod straight.

The press also kept track of John D. Rockefeller. He died in 1937, at the age of ninety-eight. The old codger had been indulging his twin passions for God and golf (and some hanky-panky with buxom ladies in horse-drawn carriages) until the Grim Reaper's icy breath frightened him into conserving his energy. His empire, though much modified, was intact, and his charitable foundation had funded vast undertakings in science, medicine, and education so munificently that it had changed the nature of philanthropy itself.

In the late 1930s, Ida overcame her long aversion and began writing her autobiography. Back in 1920 she had told Phillips, "Autobiographies are usually ridiculous in the way they avoid the person that they talk about. For most of them you might as well call four walls a house." She used Roseboro' as a critical sounding board, fretting to her old friend that the writing was like taking her clothes off in public. An early working title was *A Confession of Faith*. Someone proposed *A Woman Who Works,* and that became *All in the Day's Work.*

Ida posing with a statue of Lincoln.

Roseboro' gave her some good advice, usually with sly teasing. Bemused by the subjects Ida found interesting, she urged her not to "leave out the colorful human bits in order to spare the dead and gone." She sometimes addressed her letters to "dear and great person" and signed them "with admiration affection and scorn." Ida nearly always accepted Roseboro's revisions with gratitude, vowing she liked nothing more than "a good drubbing."

When it came to introspection, Ida hadn't progressed much beyond her early journal entries. In 1934 she had told the Pen and Brush Club that William James was her chief authority on psychology, and the annual examination she conducted of her own mind was apparently along lines he had recommended. She likened her mind to a layer cake. There was a top layer and then a second one that regularly broke through it; for example, when she gave a lecture, she might also register that a man in the audience was looking bored. She told the club that this was not anything "subconscious" but an active substratum of consciousness.

Her autobiography is wry, modest, and straightforward, revealing little more than her topmost layer. She was on familiar terms with the rich and famous of her time, but she never drops their names gratuitously. The book displays the tart common sense and discipline with which she lived and worked. She hated that her subject was herself, which clearly inhibited her. If she avoided blowing her own horn, she also found little that needed to be justified. She could lay claim to her eminence but not to any ambition that might have led to it. Naturally equipped with tremendous curiosity and energy, she had grown wise in the ways of the world and the goodness, wickedness, and folly of human beings. She had made herself, with admirable strength of character, a figure to be reckoned with. She rarely hinted at any deep emotions.

When she finished her manuscript in 1939, Ida invited Sam McClure to the National Arts Club and asked his opinion of it. He said she ought to include more of "his struggle." She gently reminded him that she was penning her life, not his, and came away feeling that Sam was surprised she had done as well as she had: "He practically told me so."

John Phillips also read a draft and was dismayed to find that he had been entirely omitted. He protested and Ida apologized profusely, wondering how she'd ever gotten into the awful business of writing the book. Money, of course, was the reason. She subsequently added Phillips to the manuscript. After the book was published, Phillips said it had no hint of ego, that Ida was "always searching; nothing human was foreign to her. With [her] abounding curiosity and interest [she] was always after the actual facts and enough of them for a usable truth."

Roseboro's final verdict was that the book was "too pious and for all its apologetical atmosphere it is too cocksure." But Ada McCormick elicited the most achingly sad review from Ray Stannard Baker. In answer to her inquiry, he wrote to her:

> I looked with hope into her autobiography but she was not there. It was all stiff and formal, a record of certain dry facts and events, not a life deeply and beautifully lived. (Women can't be shameless enough?) She could not, for instance, put into her autobiography that terrible brother of hers or her pathetic helpless family, and without them, exactly as they were, how [can we] know the greatness of her compassion or the full beauty of her life.
>
> I know exactly what it meant when she spoke of S.S. having ruined her professional life. I could enlarge on that! She was by no means the only one. S.S. had the devouring egotism of ge-

nius — feeding remorselessly upon the gifts and talents of everyone he met to serve his own ambition.

Yes, she liked me. I recall once long ago she told me of an early
romance, smilingly — it was in the Chautauqua days — it seemed
not to have been serious on her side.

Even people who knew nothing of her family and its troubles used "goodness" and "virtue" along with "moral courage" to describe Ida. It certainly
wasn't a sentimental trait. It doesn't diminish her store of virtues to observe
that her goodness could function as a protective shield. It kept her from
seeming a threat to either men or women, and it kept them at bay.

CHAPTER TWENTY

The Final Chapter

*J*DA TOLD A friend she hadn't given a thought to old age until she turned seventy-five and since then had been keeping watch on herself for signs of failing. She hoped to make it to ninety. She was in her seventies and shaking badly before she was finally moved to research the violent tremors she suffered. When she learned something about Parkinson's disease, she demanded that her doctor tell her the truth. He admitted she had it, and she responded by making adjustments so that she could go on writing even with uncontrollable — and worsening — palsy. She referred to her malady, the few times she acknowledged it, as "Mr. Parkinson."

She turned eighty on November 5, 1937. Ida and her secretary spent days opening congratulatory cards and letters and arranging flowers. Newspapers interviewed her and editorials celebrated her. The *New York Times* cited not only her unwavering devotion to truth and the insight with which she seized upon the essential and discarded the inessential, but also her "great personality." She was amazed and moved, sometimes to tears. The John Finleys, the Ray Bakers, and

Sam McClure threw a dinner in her honor. Sam, stooped but still garrulous, dominated the evening, and the others "listened as if we'd never heard the stories before." Ironically, one celebration was held in the newly opened Rockefeller Center.

Ida was making notes for another book, to be called *Life After Eighty*. Her outline included such topic heads as old age, escape (suicide), Parkinson's, Montessori for the old (techniques for mastering daily tasks with trembling fingers or loss of balance), mind and memory, facing facts, economic security, training for new jobs, late realizations about life, inner world. It was never completed.

An interview in the *New York Herald Tribune* in 1939 was titled "The World Has Confused Miss Tarbell and She Admits It." Ida announced that she had decided to attend no more dinners, to speak only at her clubs, and to give no more interviews. She wrote for three hours every day and took

Ida taught a class at Allegheny College in 1939.

her meals at the National Arts Club. She had to keep working, she said, because she didn't qualify for Social Security, probably because she had not been earning a salary.

She had lived through many depressions and panics and now was enduring the Great Depression. FDR's New Deal had done much to sustain the economy and give Americans a safety net. But Ida was suspicious of FDR, as she had been of his cousin Theodore. They were both aristocrats, impatient with sluggish process and tempted by authoritarian solutions. Ida seemed to think that was okay for Italy but not for the United States. She had always believed in gradual change, and FDR's policies looked hasty, erratic, and sometimes even illegal. She got satisfaction regularly from journalist Walter Lippmann's like-minded opinions and wept when the *New York World,* which ran his column, shut down.

Ida and Roseboro' exchanged frequent jokey notes, some of them consisting just of "wild and wavy lines." Roseboro' wrote to McCormick that Ida "seems to me to . . . get warmer as she grows older. There is a marvelous good will that emanates from her; that is the word; it is not announced, it radiates. All sorts of people I find feeling it, along with her intrinsic importance."

Ida was still assuming Will's debts and paying for his various hospitalizations and supporting his wife and his mother-in-law, as well as her own sister, Sarah. Ida employed two nieces as secretaries until their inadequacies forced her to let them go. She bought a ranch for her nephew when his foray into the oil business floundered, and she helped pay for the education of grandnephews and grandnieces.

In 1940 Ida's declining health and finances forced her to give up her New York apartment and submit to Sarah's care in Connecticut. A note in her spidery hand reads, "Mr. Parkinson is more active than normal." Sarah helped

Ida, still a towering figure in old age, visiting the New York World's Fair in 1939.

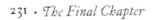

set her up on the first floor of the farmhouse and carried being her gate-keeper to a despotic extreme, allowing almost no one to see her. To spare her weakened heart, Ida was permitted to sit up for only an hour a day. Unable either to dictate or to write, she had taught herself at eighty to type with her left hand. She often used the hour allotted her to peck out a letter to John Phillips, sometimes to joke that she was braced, after America entered into a second world war, for a German invasion of Connecticut. She told him she hadn't made much progress with typing because Sarah wouldn't let her practice, and added, poignantly, "I am glad you said in your last communication you are resolute enough to lock the door on your loving family. Families never recognize privacy as an inalienable right. I think I'll put it in the Constitution for a New World I am thinking of preparing." Perhaps in all the years she'd spent trying to make it up to her hapless relatives for having achieved so much more than they, she'd never before permitted herself a complaint.

Her brother, Will, by then living elsewhere, died in 1941. Sarah invited his widow to come and live with them in the farmhouse. It wasn't what Ida wanted. She told Phillips, "I thought I had things fixed up for the rest of my life, but I seem to have upset not only my own but the family apple cart."

Ada McCormick arrived one day and breached the barricade to Ida's bedroom. Sarah removed her after a sixty-second audience. Ida's imprisonment at Sarah's hands must have driven her nearly crazy, but she managed to bear it in good humor as she had most difficulties all her life.

Ida gave Phillips an account of a visit by Sam McClure, whose daughter brought him "only for a call. He is almost gone, I think — undernourishment. White, shaky, frail. Exhausted voice, except when he speaks of Roosevelt [FDR] . . . I felt I was saying goodbye to a dying man. . . . It seems so a part of things, like the coming of fall."

Sparing Ida the exertion of seeing people didn't lengthen her life. A few days before Christmas 1943, she lapsed into a coma. She was taken to Bridgeport Hospital and died there of pneumonia on January 6, 1944. She was buried in Titusville with her parents.

A funeral was held at the First Presbyterian Church in New York City. The speaker referred to Ida's "cool, well-trained brain — the kind thought to be exclusively masculine." She was called "handsome, tastefully dressed, personally conservative, a college-educated gentlewoman who contributed to one of the biggest rough and tumble, scratch and gouge fights [the] country ever went into. . . . People referred to her double life . . . kind to those around her, taking up the cause of society . . . [and were] stimulated by the vigor of her mind and cheered by her faith in humanity."

Ida left the farm to her sister, and it is now a national historic landmark.

She, who had lost so many friends in early middle age, was the first of her close *McClure's* colleagues to go. A year later, Viola Roseboro' lay near death on Staten Island. One day she opened her eyes and beheld Sam McClure. Seeing that she was conscious, he launched into a summary of the history of human freedom he was writing. Roseboro' had kept John Phillips away because she didn't want him to see her as a frowsy, disheveled old crone. But Phillips disobeyed and came in time to say goodbye. Roseboro' is buried in the cemetery of the sanitarium at Clifton Springs.

A few months after Ida died, Sam tottered to the stage at the Union League Club in New York City to receive the Medal of Merit from the National Institute of Arts and Letters in recognition of the creation, with Ida and the other muckrakers, of a new kind of journalism in *McClure's*. "The American people owe a great debt to this man once famous, now almost forgotten," said the president of the institute. Sam lived a few years longer, finally lapsing into confusion. On February 28, 1949, he was told that eighty-seven-year-old John Phillips was gone. On March 21, Sam McClure, ninety-two, followed his oldest friend.

———— ✳ ————

In her time, Ida M. Tarbell was the only woman doing investigative reporting. She began when women were entering the work force for the first time in great numbers, usually as clerks and office workers, not as byline writers. Her breakthrough achievement was foreshadowed by her early life; she prepared herself to be exactly what she became, even though the category didn't exist during her childhood and youth.

She would be dismayed to know that her name is forever linked to "muckraker," the term she rejected. She considered herself a historian who exposed threats to traditional institutions that she believed were vital for democracy and the pursuit of happiness. She feared that corporate success at any price threatened social equality and gave money a morbid importance. Her righteousness was tempered by modesty, charm, and compassion. Once she had taken the leap and declared herself a writer, she responded to events and trends by writing about them. Her career as a writer and then as a reluctant public figure was marked by unwavering honesty.

Her vision had some blind spots, most notably her "limitation of mind," as Jane Addams had put it, in regard to women. As the virtuous small-town society she loved lost its character and beauty to industrialism and the race for wealth, she thought women could save it by nurturing family values. To that end, she urged them to stay home. Such a position is surprising in someone capable of both sympathy and trenchant analysis. Given Ida's belief that work was the source of life's meaning, it is downright amazing. She didn't "get" the woman question, and "limitation of mind" is a useful phrase for describing the prejudice and condescension that hobbled her. Had she thrown her intellect and reputation behind full citizenship for women, her other achievements would surely be more celebrated now.

For a woman to cling to celibacy while maintaining vital friendships with men and women was less unusual in Ida's time than it would be today. Then, single working women often set up households together, sometimes in "Boston marriages," which might include sex. Ida denied herself physical relations — she probably didn't even hug — and her emotional connections seem to have been limited, if occasionally fervent. She was outspoken about having sacrificed a normal existence for the sake of her career. This choice probably blinded her, especially to the full range of the woman question. She primly credited women with an intuitive comprehension of the human condition, but she herself focused narrowly on maintaining the status quo, rather than on achieving full citizenship for all.

Without regulation of the trusts, would the United States have been sooner or later ruled by an emperor, as the president of Yale warned in 1901? Other reformers, such as Henry Demarest Lloyd, investigated Standard Oil, and the mood of the nation had begun to turn against trusts by the time Ida took up her pen. But it was her work that electrified the nation and was the catalyst for government regulation. She helped invent investigative journalism and was probably its most incorruptible practitioner, recording history and changing it in the process.

Inequality of opportunity and grossly lopsided distribution of wealth, rapacious profit-chasing, shady financial instruments, and campaign contributions still threaten our democracy. The crusading journalists who address them are the professional descendants of Ida M. Tarbell.

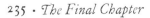

Author's Note

When I was growing up in the 1950s, Ida M. Tarbell had been forgotten by most of America, but her name was frequently heard in my home. My parents had met as undergraduates at Knox College, in Galesburg, Illinois. Growing up in Tulsa, Oklahoma, my father was a boy journalist, reporting for the two major newspapers. He was proud of the muckraking achievements of Knox's graduates Sam McClure, John Phillips, and John H. Finley — and, by extension, of Ida M. Tarbell. She received an honorary doctorate from Knox shortly before I was born. When I began reading her letters at Allegheny College, I discovered that my father had written to her once and that she had replied.

I was young during the era that fell ignominiously between the first wave of feminism (the struggle for women's suffrage) and its second wave (in the 1970s). Thus, Ida Tarbell, a woman who made it in a man's world by working hard and remaining inoffensive, was one of my few models for how to succeed. After I began my career, that model was rightly despised. No more would women have to insinuate themselves into a world made by men; the world itself would have to change. Or so we dreamed. Ida can still be admired, but she also has to be explained. That's what I set out to do in this book.

Acknowledgments

I am very grateful to Jane Westenfeld of the Ida M. Tarbell Collection, Pelletier Library, Allegheny College, for her great help and patience. Ruth Andel, archivist at Allegheny, helped with photographs. Sheri Hamilton, executive director, and Susan Beates, historian, curator at the Drake Well Museum, also made crucial materials available. Thanks also to the staff at the Sophia Smith Collection, Smith College; Janice Sands, executive director of the Pen and Brush Club; David K. Frasier and his staff at the Lilly Library, University of Indiana; and Charlotte V. Priddle of Fales Library, New York University. Dinah Stevenson, publisher, Clarion Books, copyeditor Alexandra Redmond, and editorial assistant Anna Dobbin gave the manuscript tough, sensitive, comprehensive editing that improved it immeasurably.

Source Notes

ABBREVIATIONS

All: All in the Day's Work, Tarbell's autobiography.

Allegheny: The Ida M. Tarbell Collection, Pelletier Library, Allegheny College, Meadville, Pennsylvania.

Drake: The Ida M. Tarbell Papers, the Drake Well Museum, Titusville, Pennsylvania.

IMT: Ida M. Tarbell.

journal: IMT's journal of May 1905–April 1906, transcribed by Kate Wayland-Smith, Allegheny.

Smith: The Ida M. Tarbell Collection, Sophia Smith Library, Smith College, Northampton, Massachusetts.

All other sources are either provided in full or cited by author name with a complete reference in the bibliography.

Letters are from IMT unless otherwise noted.

CHAPTER 1. THE OIL REGION

4 "from . . . together": *All,* 3.

5 It took him . . . as he went: Lewis Gannett, *New York Herald Tribune,* April 18, 1939, says Franklin walked 180 miles before he found a school that would pay him enough to purchase rides the rest of the way.

7 spring pole: a flexible pole on a fulcrum. Using a spring pole, two men could

cheaply drill down three feet in a day. See Samuel T. Pees, "Oil History," Oil History website, www.petroleumhistory.org/OilHistory/pages/Cable/kicking.html.

11 "No industry . . . petroleum": *All,* 9.

13 "peace . . . curiosity," "belonged . . . floated": *All,* 7.

CHAPTER 2. BURNING CURIOSITY

15–16 "The relics . . . away": *All,* 9.

16 "heard . . . curiosity": *All,* 11.
she began to scream: Brady, 13.
"It changed . . . hills": Letter to Nettie Grumbine, August 14, 1934, Allegheny.
"The change . . . families": Letter to Nettie Grumbine, August 14, 1934, Allegheny.

19 "feed [her] curiosity . . . know": *All,* 15.

20 "Let . . . Center": Letter to Nettie Grumbine, August 14, 1934, Allegheny.
"the orgies . . . combined": Dolson, 132.
"I . . . life": quoted in Brady, 12.

21 "[the Tarbells] never . . . father": *All,* 18.

CHAPTER 3. DEFINING HERSELF

23–24 "keenly . . . heart": *All,* 16.

26 "I suppose . . . pupil": *All,* 21
"Suddenly . . . offer": *All,* 21.
"A Bible . . . on": *All,* 27.

27 "I had . . . ruin": *All,* 28.

28 saved her money: From odd jobs or allowance — she doesn't say which.
Around this time, Ida asked her father for one hundred dollars to invest in the Oil Exchange and he angrily refused, saying that no daughter of his would gamble. Brady, 21.

29 "useless and destructive": Barry Werth, *Banquet at Delmonico's* (New York: Random House, 2009), 26.
She found nothing of the sort: *All,* 28. Both Darwin and Spencer wrestled in print over the origin of moral behavior. They disagreed, Spencer asserting that

moral attitudes were inherited, Darwin that they are learned. Charles Darwin, *The Descent of Man* (New York: W. W. Norton, 2006), 832–35.

"show them": *All,* 66.

"for any special . . . Chautauqua": *All,* 66.

"The quest . . . quests": Letter, quoted in Brady, 20.

30–31 The *Police Gazette* ran more . . . poses: Amanda Frisken, *Victoria Woodhull's Sexual Revolution* (Philadelphia: University of Pennsylvania Press, 2004), 16.

CHAPTER 4. THE BIRTH OF THE OCTOPUS

33 "involved . . . enterprises": Rockefeller, 33.

34 "these . . . Creator": Chernow, 76.

35 "frugality . . . expansion": Chernow, 85.

37 "suddenly . . . eyes": *All,* 23.

He personally turned down . . . oil: Dolson, 267.

38 "cooperation": Chernow, 154.

"In that fine fight [against the SIC] . . . of one": *All,* 26.

39 "looking pretty blue": Stiles, 264.

39–40 "In walking . . . struggle": *All,* 26.

CHAPTER 5. AN EDUCATION

41 "delightful and entertaining": *All,* 35.

42 "prove . . . vicinity": *All,* 35.

"I could . . . suffering": *Allegheny Monthly* 27, no. 1 (1922): 4.

"Lost . . . Boy": *All,* 40.

44 "There would . . . it": Cotkin, 78.

"one crisis . . . minced . . . Grecian bend": IMT, "I Remember," interview with Frederick Tisdale, ms., Allegheny.

45 The boys at Allegheny . . . as well: Helmreich, 13.

"a dangerous feat": IMT, "I Remember," Allegheny.

"Look inside": *All,* 42.

46 "slimy . . . loathsome": *All,* 43.

"Some day . . . Boston!": *All,* 44.

47 "She was too . . . people": Brady, 28.

"meagre," "the matter . . . art": Helmreich, 15.

Margaret Fuller Ossoli (1810–1850) was a writer, educator, editor, activist, and friend to transcendentalists Ralph Waldo Emerson and Henry David Thoreau.

49 "a grotesque . . . fallacies": Helmreich, 13.

"engaged . . . married": Brady, 30.

"calling . . . God": Brady, 31.

CHAPTER 6. A JOB AND A CALLING

50 "If I had been . . . curious": *All,* 49.

50–51 "in many . . . time," "a fine . . . 1880s," "direct . . . everything" : *All,* 54.

52 "The destruction . . . work": *All,* 56.

53 "retreat": *All,* 49.

54–55 "Women's desire for . . . education": *All,* 70.

55 "girl Friday": a general assistant, after Man Friday in Defoe's *Robinson Crusoe.*

56 "a virtually . . . America," "lavish . . . poor": Trachtenberg, 143.

"great revolts," "forgotten . . . 1880s," "terrible . . . hands": IMT, talk at Pen and Brush Club on death of Jane Addams, 1935, ms., Allegheny.

57 "If the master . . . disaster": Lears, *No Place of Grace,* 29.

"It seemed . . . ruin": quoted in Trachtenberg, 71.

58–59 "For the first . . . loving work," "Will . . . Will," "The Trail . . . agin him," "[A]ll . . . Poultry": IMT, *Chautauqua Journal,* 1885, Allegheny.

59 "Having . . . doing": *All,* 75.

59–60 "Morally . . . learn": IMT, "The Arts and Industries of Cincinnati," 162.

61 "I had been . . . campaign": *All,* 75.

"Power . . . home": *All,* 75.

62 "she must . . . womanhood": Brady, 37.

"going . . . route": IMT, "The Disillusionment of Women," ms., Allegheny.

"large . . . times": S. Weinberg, 122.

"There . . . vote": S. Weinberg, 122.

64   "know . . . behind them": Chautauqua folder, Allegheny.

     "I long . . . utmost": Letter from William James to his wife, July 31, 1896, www.archive.org/stream/thelettersofwill02jameuoft/thelettersofwill02jameuoft_djvu txt.

64–65   "Ouf . . . uninspiring": Brady, 41.

65   "effeminate . . . heroism": Trachtenberg, 141.

     "The tumults . . . them": *All,* 81.

     "You're . . . respectability!" *All,* 79.

66   French prose: IMT probably read critic W. C. Brownell's influential "French Traits," *Scribner's* (February 1889), which contrasted the French "social instinct" with the American celebration of individualism. Brownell attributed the clarity of French prose to France's public culture, to which all citizens subscribed. There was a "common ground" in France of belief in the high value of intellectual discussion.

     "Flood said . . . knew it": *All,* 87.

     "It was . . . strength": *All,* 88.

67   "You'll starve!": *All,* 87.

     "beheading in Meadville": Letter to her family, fall 1893, Allegheny.

     "I don't care . . . ways": quoted in S. Weinberg, 125.

     "I wanted freedom": *All,* 86.

CHAPTER 7. PARIS

IMT's letters to her family from Paris, quoted in this chapter, are in the Ada Pierce McCormick Collection, University of Arizona, Tucson. Transcriptions of the letters are in Allegheny.

68   "I Fall in Love": *All,* 89.

     "thousand . . . tradition": Henry James, *The American Scene* (New York and London: Harper & Brothers, 1907), 321.

     "I have become . . . basin," "You must . . . Europe": Kochersberger, 22.

     "the people are not . . . people": Letter to her family, August 25, 1891, Allegheny.

69   "my sweetheart," "lady love": numerous letters.

"scorn it": Kochersberger, 26.

"From . . . literature": Brady, 55.

"The people . . . absolutely," "They . . . jeer them": Letter to her family, November 13, 1891, Allegheny.

71 "But here . . . write it": Letter to her family, November 1891.

73 A story she wrote . . . any joy: IMT, "The Compatriot," *New England Magazine,* 1894, discussed in Brady, 79–80.

74 "I've just . . . tonight!": All sources repeat this story. *All,* 118–19.

76 "said to his partner . . . magazine' ": Lyon, 117.

77 "Fool! . . . money!": *All,* 119.

"hustler," "enthusiasm . . . through," "good joke," "the Mogul . . . in it": Letter to her family, summer 1892.

"My work . . . New York": Letter to her family, August 8, 1892, Allegheny.

"I am . . . friends": Letter to her family, August 8, 1892, Allegheny.

While hoping . . . not to: Ida's skeptical attitude was in contrast to that of Willa Cather, who was recruited by Sam McClure in 1906. He published Cather's stories and convinced her to work for him as an editor. After their first dazzling interview, she felt transformed by his enthusiasm. Outside, she kept an eye out for streetcars, feeling too valuable to risk being run down. As an editor, Cather was at the center of literary life, but she tried repeatedly to leave in order to write. To keep her in harness, McClure belittled her fiction and she lost confidence as a writer for several years. Sharon O'Brien, *Willa Cather* (Cambridge, Mass.: Harvard University Press, 1997), 271–72, 288–93.

CHAPTER 8. EDGING TOWARD HOME

IMT's letters to her family from Paris, quoted in this chapter, are in the Ada Pierce McCormick Collection, University of Arizona, Tucson. Transcriptions of the letters are in Allegheny.

79 "the miserable . . . Will!": Letter to her family, October 16, 1892.

"lift": *All,* 160.

80 "Jealousy . . . meets," "usefulness," "self-denying . . . role": Brady, 67.

"This is . . . journalist": IMT, "Pasteur at Home," 333.

81 "pluck . . . writing," "sincere . . . writing," "a ripened . . . practice," "It is not . . . following": Brady, 68.

"It meant . . . journalism": *All,* 122.

82 "pay . . . bill": Letter to her family, fall 1893.

"my . . . existence": Letter to her family, no date.

"Of course . . . bounced": Letter to her family, 1892.

83 "I had undertaken . . . stress": *All,* 142.

"The reasonable . . . demands": IMT, *Madame Roland,* 132.

"This woman . . . upset": *All,* 143.

"It was . . . logic": IMT, *Madame Roland,* 133.

84 "reactionist": Letter to Alice French, quoted in Brady, 78.

"intuitions . . . on," "no party . . . violence": *All,* 142–43.

84–85 "As usual . . . write me," "If McClure . . . this time": Brady, 83.

85–86 "He could . . . vitality": Lyon, 16–17.

86 "while . . . cathedrals": *All,* 145. At this time, IMT's future friends Elizabeth Marbury and Elsie de Wolfe were conducting a salon in their home on Irving Place.

CHAPTER 9. McCLURE'S

87 "Where . . . tonight?": Lyon, 84.

88 "From the looks . . . schoolmarm," "She . . . write!": Lyon, 117.

"knew . . . style": *All,* 158.

89 "What . . . get on!": Sedgwick, 142.

"It throbs . . . end": *The Review of Reviews,* quoted in Mott, 596.

"blew . . . genius," "honesty . . . soul," "the power . . . go": White, 200. Gardiner Hubbard was Alexander Graham Bell's father-in-law.

90 "It was . . . try?": *All,* 148.

91 "That eagerness . . . geniuses": Lyon, 133.

92 "the greatest . . . own": IMT, "Napoleon Bonaparte," April 1895.

"tongue . . . sketch": *All,* 151.

93 "[The] sketch . . . topsy-turvy": *All,* 153.

94   "as eager . . . hunt": *All,* 154.

"a string . . . editors": *All,* 160.

"nose for humbug," "patience . . . impatient": *All,* 156.

"Out . . . Report": Lyon, 134

95   "They got . . . Lincoln": Lyon, 135.

"I would not . . . unknown": *All,* 164.

96   "few of them . . . gifts": IMT, quoted in *The Bookman* 16 (1903): 440.

John H. Finley: As president of City College, beginning in 1903 he recruited the children of immigrants on the Lower East Side to its student body when other schools were using quotas to keep them out.

"the stirring . . . sought": *All,* 171.

97–98   "the values . . . nation": Tomkins, 50.

typewriter: Smith has a receipt for a Remington typewriter and carbon ribbons purchased in 1899, presumably for IMT's secretary.

99   "jeered," "the simple . . . truth": Lincoln's Funeral, *McClure's,* September 1899, 454.

101   "the wild editor": Steffens, 361.

CHAPTER 10. AN IMPERIAL NATION

102   Rockefeller gave $250,000 to McKinley, a huge sum for the period.

"In strict . . . one": Zinn, 297. The philosopher William James later called, instead, for "the moral equivalent to war" — strenuous *peaceful* activity that would restore the manliness of Americans. www.constitution.org/wj/meow.htm.

"All great . . . war": Zinn, 300.

104   "like . . . skates": *All,* 189.

"You . . . serve it?," "Between . . . resigned": *All,* 195.

105   "one . . . ourselves": Beatty, 387.

106   "Educate . . . them," "went . . . soundly": Zinn, 313.

"Chiefly . . . McClure crowd": *All,* 153.

108   "I was deeply . . . on it": Letter to Roseboro', February 21, 1934, Allegheny.

"have . . . Garden": Lyon, 192.

110   "McClure was . . . integrity": Lyon, 152.

"Miss Tarbell . . . else": Baker, 80.

111 "Spartan": *All,* 198.

CHAPTER 11. FINDING A MISSION

113 "the wolf . . . door": Wilson, 101.
Neurasthenia is discussed in Lutz.

114 "So far . . . hitherto": Letter from Hazen to IMT, 1899, Allegheny.
"look after . . . world": Letter from Hazen to IMT, January 24, 1900, Smith.
"ordeal": Letter, February 1900, Smith.

114–15 "her life . . . off," "She seemed . . . at all": Brady, 115.

115 "You are . . . analysis": Letter from Hazen to IMT, August 14, 1899, Allegheny.
"I want . . . love": Letter from McClure to IMT, April 14, 1900, Allegheny.
"If Miss Tarbell . . . by": Steffens, 393.
"avenues . . . were not": McClure, 265.

118 "that [the articles] . . . cities": Lyon, 179.
"carefully . . . life": Burton Raffel, *Politicians, Poets, and Con Men* (Hamden,
Conn.: Archon, 1986), 118.
middle-class sensibilities: Richard Watson Gilder, editor of the *Century,*
demanded that Mark Twain make cuts in *Huckleberry Finn,* as his writing was
sometimes "inartistically and indefensibly coarse." Lyon, 68.

118–19 "anything . . . bliss!": Lyon, 151.

120 "The great . . . circulation": Lyon, 176.

121 "combining . . . way": Lyon, 191.

122 "hadn't . . . method": *All,* 205.
"I want . . . time!": Lyon, 194.
"give . . . few": IMT, *The History of the Standard Oil Company,* vol. 1, 3.
"a doubtful . . . *McClure's*": *All,* 206.

123 "courage . . . of?": *All,* 206.

CHAPTER 12. MUCKRAKERS TOGETHER

127 In "The Shame of the Cities," Steffens coined the term "the system" to

describe the synergies that bred corruption — for example, police and criminals cooperating in ways that preserved their power.

128 "He was the least . . . them": S. Weinberg, 195–96.
"it might have caused . . . children'": Steffens, 393.
"She was another . . . unreliable": Brady, 136.

129 "tight-fisted . . . expansion": Chernow, 85
"Godlike," "the angel . . . mercy," "Moses": Chernow, 153.

130 "Rockefeller . . . Clam": Chernow, 426.
"kiss . . . vehemently": Chernow, 295.
"the most . . . conceived": Beatty, 386.
"done . . . refine it": Chernow, 266.

131 "constantly . . . animal": Chernow, 299.

133 "a persistent . . . fear": *All,* 207.
"Don't . . . magazine": *All,* 207.
"they": Brady, 123.

134 "Things . . . *stick*": Lyon, 199.

135 "handsomest . . . laughter": *All,* 212–13.

136 "I think . . . rain": *All,* 218.
"that . . . escape": *All,* 216.

137 "Where . . . stuff?," "You know . . . authentic": *All,* 227.

CHAPTER 13. SIDDALL

The Tarbell-Siddall correspondence recounting their research for *The History of the Standard Oil Company* is at the Drake Well Museum, Titusville, Pennsylvania. All quotes in this chapter are from letters in the collection, unless otherwise noted.

138 Ray Baker thought that Siddall, "with his round face, his round mouth, & his round eyes, spoofing at human nature," was disliked by the *McClure's* staff. Wilson, note, 98.
"all discretion . . . with": Letter to John Siddall, September 1901.

139 "Standard . . . land": Letter from Siddall to Bert Boyden, September 15, 1901.

140 "It's . . . novel": Siddall to IMT, September 22, 1902.

"There is . . . establishment!": Letter to Siddall, May 12, 1902.

"winks . . . documents": Chernow, lecture at Leon Levy Biography Center, CUNY, New York, September 28, 2010.

"One day . . . surface": "The History of the Standard Oil Company," *McClure's,* November 1902, 5.

141–42 "They came . . . future": "The History of the Standard Oil Company," *McClure's,* November 1902, 16.

"an arraignment . . . character," " 'The . . . Law' ": *McClure's,* January 1903, reproduced in tarbell.allegheny.edu/mc2.html.

"There . . . liberty": *McClure's,* January 1903.

143 "I regret . . . do": Rockefeller, 107.

"As the work . . . moment": Letter to Siddall, December 17, 1902.

144 "It . . . Barrel": Letter to Siddall, June 18, 1902.

"Old Dr. . . . him": Letter from Siddall to IMT, May 2, 1903, Drake.

manhunt: Chernow, 461.

144–45 "was warding . . . week," "Doesn't . . . hypocrisy?" "I am much . . . years": Letter to Siddall, June 18, 1903.

145 "the most dangerous . . . life": Chernow, 440.

146 Rockefeller's Sunday school was also a target of Mark Twain's. In Twain's words, Rockefeller was "Admiral" of a Sunday school, where he "explained how he got his dollars . . . [the audience] listened in rapture and divided its worship between him and his Creator — unequally." These talks were "telegraphed about the country." Mark Twain, *Autobiography of Mark Twain,* vol. 1 (Berkeley, California: University of California Press, 2010), 421.

"the oldest . . . power!" *All,* 235.

"my lady friend": Chernow, xxi. Rockefeller allowed himself to vent on the subject of IMT's accusations in an extended interview for an authorized biography. After its author had worked on it for seven years, Rockefeller's son, John D. Rockefeller Jr., took the manuscript to IMT for her review. She pronounced it evasive and recommended against publication. It was put away in the Rockefeller archives. The younger Rockefeller and IMT enjoyed mutual respect and even some affection. Chernow, 619.

147 "Do you . . . hard work?": Rockefeller, 5.

"It is . . . resent it": Brady, 148; Lyon, 259.

"menace," "the most . . . money," "live in the dark": IMT, "John D. Rockefeller: A Character Study," July 1905, 227.

147–48 "Why . . . regard": IMT, "John D. Rockefeller: A Character Study," July 1905, 249.

149 "concentration . . . repulsive," "a living mummy," "There . . . Rockefeller," "cult . . . unpretentious," "completing . . . nation," "if . . . money": IMT, "John D. Rockefeller: A Character Study," August 1905, 388–89.

How did Ida . . . trust?: In a lecture at the Leon Levy Biography Center, CUNY, New York, September 28, 2010, Chernow called IMT's *History* "the most impressive thing ever written [about Standard Oil]" and recounted his own frustration while conducting research in the Rockefeller papers.

150 "The way . . . of you": Brady, 148.

151 "Ida . . . kill": Elbert Hubbard, *The Standard Oil Company* (East Aurora, N.Y.: Ryecrofters, 1910), 14, www.books.google.com/books?id=1fYJAAAAIAAJ&printsec=frontcover#v=onepage&q&f=false.

"Hysterical . . . Fact": clipping in a scrapbook kept by IMT, Allegheny.

"I was . . . means," "legitimate greatness," "There was not . . . for me": *All,* 230.

152 "exposed . . . journalism," "[the] ignorance . . . problems": Wilson, 198. "They were making a magazine for our kind — the literate middle class," exulted William Allen White of *McClure's.* White, 300.

CHAPTER 14. AN UNHINGED BOSS

153 "In buying . . . her out": Lyon, 258.

154 "surrounded by spinsters," "degenerate . . . incurable": Lyon, 262.

154 "I took . . . not be": Lyon, 261.

154–55 "Is there . . . feelings": Lyon, 264.

155 "My Dear . . . Miss Wilkinson": Brady, 161–62.

"easy . . . loneliness": Brady, 167.

155 "all right," "I've been . . . together": Lyon, 263.

"it would . . . madness," "heart . . . heart," "long . . . excitement": Lyon, 264.

155–56 "While . . . soul": Lyon, 264.

156   "notion": Lyon, 266–67.

       "tired": Lyon, 270.

       "I have always . . . her": Lyon, 276.

157   "500 . . . at C": IMT's folder marked "L'affaire," Allegheny.

       extortion: In an extended essay based on the Tarbell papers, Allegheny
       student Greg Gross surmises that this refers to hush money. Greg Gross,
       " 'The Explosions of Our Fine Idealistic Undertakings': The Staff Breakup of
       McClure's Magazine," tarbell-Allegheny.edu.mctable.html.

       "Idarem . . . Jawn D": Brady, 174.

       "There . . . explored": journal.

158   "fifty . . . alone": *All,* 247.

159   "They . . . papers": Letter to Boyden, April 4, 1905, Smith.

       "He all right": *All,* 248.

       "The worst . . . fact," "approve my apostasy": Letter from Hazen to IMT,
       December 4, 1900, Allegheny.

159–60   "If I . . . experience": journal.

160   "wise . . . unattainable," "comprehension," "great visage," "big . . . sweet," "hardly
       . . . writings," "a soul . . . cathedral," "I let . . . them," "rudeness . . . inartisteness,"
       "blushed," "sitting near [James]": journal.

161   "leaped . . . pitiful I am": journal.

       "felt . . . life," "independently . . . creator," "there is . . . he or she": Henry James,
       The Question of Our Speech; The Lesson of Balzac: Two Lectures (Boston:
       Houghton Mifflin, 1905), www.archive.org/stream/
       questionourspee00jamegoog/questionourspee00jamegoog_djvu.txt.

161–62   "I see it . . . interpret life," *"I hope you . . . Miss!"* "great," "She has . . .
       personality," "This is . . . myself," "Our friendship . . . strong," "too fluttering . . .
       him," "funk of soul," "end of HJ," "Cherish . . . elbow!": journal.

162   "noise . . . by it": journal.

CHAPTER 15. THE AMERICAN MAGAZINE

163   "My dear . . . magazine": Letter from McClure to IMT, December 30, 1901.

       "better . . . time": Letter to McClure, October 18, 1904, Allegheny.

164 "we *can* secede": Brady, 172.

165 "He referred . . . dreadfully," "At end . . . right": Brady, 173.

"spark-plug . . . department," "I cannot . . . *cannot*": Lyon, 290–91.

166 commissioned: Details of the deal can be found in Wilson, 168–89, and Lyon, 283–93.

"Truth . . . Machiavellianism": IMT, "Commercial Machiavellianism," 5.

"derelicts . . . job": *All,* 258.

"Ethical . . . Trust," "human vultures," "benevolent," "joke": "Miss Tarbell Sees a Revolution Coming," *New York Times,* April 12, 1906, query.nytimes.com/mem /archive-free/pdf?res=F10616FA3A5A12738DDDAB0994DC405B868CF1D3.

167 "joyous reading": promotion for the *American Magazine,* Allegheny.

"the ringmaster . . . show": Baker, quoted in Boyden, 29.

"Was . . . exploded?": Letter to Baker, October 17, 1939, Allegheny.

"It is unfortunate . . . crime," "put more sky . . . landscapes": Brady, 174.

Sam McClure wanted IMT to investigate the U.S. Senate, but the turmoil at the magazine prevented it. Lyon, 274.

168 "There are beautiful . . . fellows": Theodore Roosevelt, "The Man with the Muckrake" (speech, Washington, D.C., April 15, 1906), www.theodore-roosevelt.com/images/research/txtspeeches/189.txt.

"I had hoped . . . muckrakers": *All,* 242.

168–69 "malefactors of great wealth," "muckrakers of great wealth," "malefactors," "revolt," "facts": *All,* 242.

169 "practical": *All,* 242.

"wrong . . . man": Roosevelt, 170.

"I do not admire . . . the like": Letter from Theodore Roosevelt to Sir George Trevelyan, April 10, 1907, Allegheny.

"convinced . . . country": Letter from Theodore Roosevelt to a friend, September 21, 1907, Allegheny.

170 20 percent of the wealth: *New York Times,* January 6, 1907.

"It is quite characteristic . . . disregard": Letter from Seldon Baker Esq. to Lanier Esq., November 3, 1909, Allegheny.

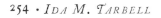

CHAPTER 16. MATERFAMILIAS

171 "Of course . . . cured": IMT remembrance in Boyden, 15.

173–74 "a very business-like . . . like men": Lewis, 237–38; Brady, 198.

174 gross inequalities in wealth: Tomkins, 97.

175 "Mr. Aldrich's 'Protection' . . . opportunity": *American Magazine,* quoted in Tomkins, 99–100.

177 "starved for her": Brady, 186.

177–78 "We need a quality . . . else is": Letter to Boyden, quoted in Lyon, 311.

178 "I think we had . . . to us": Letter to Roseboro', September 14, 1938, Allegheny. Roseboro' replied that IMT should not reveal the full story of the breakup in her autobiography, presumably referring to McClure's alleged affairs. Letter from Roseboro', undated, Allegheny.

CHAPTER 17. THE WOMAN QUESTION

181 "better than men . . . corruption": *All,* 328.

"vulgarizing," "undermine . . . manners": IMT, "The American Woman," ms., Allegheny.

"overemphasizes . . . 'door mat theory'": *All,* ms., Allegheny.

"that you . . . whole": quoted in Camhi, 163.

183 "It is not bigotry . . . thing," "early disturbers . . . peace," "No woman . . . peace": IMT, "The Uneasy Woman," in *The Business of Being a Woman,* www.gutenberg.org/files/16577/16577-8.txt.

"never . . . anything": IMT, *The Ways of Woman* (manuscript), Smith.

184 "essential barrenness . . . living," "brilliant. . . is repellent": IMT, "On the Imitation of Man," in *The Business of Being a Woman,* www.gutenberg.org/files/16577/16577-8.txt.

"A few women . . . human core": IMT, "On the Ennobling of the Woman's Business," in *The Business of Being a Woman,* www.gutenberg.org/files/16577/16577-8.txt.

"To hold . . . earth": IMT, *The Ways of Woman,* 45.

185 "I have done it . . . than I am": Brady, 202.

186–87 "I have always . . . try" and all other quotes through "You will gather . . . systems": IMT-Phillips exchange, Brady, 206–7.

187 "There is some limitation . . . mind": Brady, 203.

"to be . . . without the ballot": IMT-Phillips exchange, Brady, 206–7.

"Let us be glad . . . obligation": Brady, 207.

188 "not appall," "Women . . . change": IMT, *The Ways of Woman,* 45.

"unproductive . . . parasitical," "happiness . . . living": IMT, "The Irresponsible Woman and the Friendless Child," 1912, ms., Smith.

190 "myth . . . failure": ms., October 1924, Smith.

"since Lincoln": ms., October 1924, Smith.

She had expected . . . happened: Interview in *Literary Digest,* April 26, 1930, Smith.

191 "Death . . . Lord": Tomkins, 107.

On Taylorism, see Frederick Winslow Taylor, *The Principles of Scientific Management*, 1911, www.ibiblio.org/eldritch/fwt/ti.html and www.fordham.edu/halsall/mod/1911taylor.html. Some of the later history of the movement is entertainingly told by Jill Lepore in "Not So Fast," *New Yorker,* October 12, 2009, 114.

192 "the natural task," "to dignify . . . that task": IMT, *The Business of Being a Woman,* www.gutenberg.org/files/16577/16577-8.txt.

"Taylor believed . . . limitless": *All,* 293.

CHAPTER 18. FAMOUS

195 "Miss Tarbell's exposé . . . woman": Brady, 195.

195–96 "I cannot bear . . . is in": Brady, 209.

196 "waffled": Brady, 196.

"Give Teddy . . . good": Brady, 195.

"The progressives . . . bothered about": Letter to Boyden, August 24, 1912, Smith.

197 "I never saw . . . run": Brady, 208.

198 "I wanted to laugh . . . before," "a part . . . thing": Brady, 207.

199 "The only emotions . . . out": Brady, 208.

moving train: A special committee of the House of Representatives to investigate the Taylor system and other systems of shop management met in 1911–12 and elicited testimony from workers who were exhausted from trying to meet Taylor's arbitrary standards. Lepore, "Not So Fast," 117.

200 "a growing desire . . . justice": *New York Times,* January 20, 1915.

201 "All my pretty tales. . . them": *All,* 305.

202 "definiteness," "Her whole appearance . . . sinner": Tomkins, 113.

204 "You see . . . after suffrage": Letter from Roseboro' to IMT, September 14, 1938, Allegheny.

205 "almost amazingly . . . sense": *New York Times,* April 6, 1919.

208 Walter Lippmann called Mencken "the most powerful personal influence on this whole generation of educated people." Quoted in Warren Sloat, *1929: America Before the Crash* (New York: Macmillan, 1979), 6.

"Human affairs . . . character": *All,* 407.

"Standardization . . . ideals": *All,* 396.

209 "You will . . . age!": Brady, 225.

Ray Baker wrote Ida . . . new material: Letter from Baker to IMT, March 15, 1923, and letter to Baker, March 27, 1923, Allegheny. On September 26, 1926, the *New York Times* announced an auction of a rare first edition of the *History.* It noted that people had erroneously believed that Standard Oil had bought up and destroyed the plates when the first edition went out of print. But the plates had reverted to IMT, as per her contract with *McClure's.* Offshore book pirates had made copies and sold them. This does not address the matter of the book's unavailability in libraries.

CHAPTER 19. BUSINESS REDEEMED

210 "interesting": Brady, 236.

211 Will had already become . . . neighborhood: Letter to her lawyer, January 9, 1929, Allegheny.

"keeping . . . hall": note to Dr. Wadsworth, 1929, Allegheny.

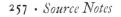

"living proof . . . changes," "same brilliance . . . makeup": Letter from Boyden to IMT, January 10, 1921, Allegheny.

212 "I personally know of . . . done": Lyon, 394.

"As I look at him . . . enthusiasm": Brady, 233.

213 The series was reviewed in the *Nation:* The critics' responses are summarized in Tomkins, 136–39. The *Nation* quote is a sign of Freud's influence on popular discourse.

214 "rescued," "ranks . . . place them": *All,* 386.

215 must have wept: Or sneered; a critic called it "distinguished by an almost incredibly even vulgarity and ineptitude." Mott, 606.

building frenzies of the twenties: Many of America's suburbs were created at this time, built in "Venetian" or other fanciful styles in imitation of houses in escapist Florida.

216 "We do the same thing . . . know": *All,* 379.

217 "Here was one . . . a lot": Brady, 240.

"awful lawlessness . . . speech," "Platonic," "got poets out . . . do it": Letter to Roseboro', February 21, 1934, Allegheny.

218 "thrift, hard work . . . purchase": *All,* 384. Mussolini ruthlessly invaded Ethiopia in 1935.

"IMT is a mighty poor . . . gratitude": Roseboro' to Phillips, August 19, 1928, quoted in Graham, 128.

"Life isn't interesting . . . idle," "do their part . . . works": IMT, talk at Whiting Hall, Knox College, November 1928, ms., Allegheny.

IMT and Hoover believed that if the reforms they recommended had been instituted, the nation would have been prepared for the shock of 1929. *All,* 375.

219 "the possessor of a keen mind . . . two of them": *New York Herald Tribune,* April 1, 1928, Smith.

"Women's equality . . . protectors": *Collier's,* September 15, 1928, quoted in Tomkins, 143–44.

"Centralized wealth . . . arrogance": IMT, *The Nationalizing of Business,* xiii.

221 "the maldistribution of wealth . . . hands": *The Nationalizing of Business,* 249.

222 "[Ida] gives me little . . . listener": Roseboro', quoted in Graham, 258.

223 "never spoke unkindly . . . tongue": Graham, 258.

On John D. Rockefeller in carriages, see Chernow, 634.

"Autobiographies are usually . . . house": Letter to Phillips, December 16, 1920, Smith.

225 "leave out the colorful . . . gone," "dear . . . person," "with admiration . . . scorn": Letter from Roseboro' to IMT, 1938, Allegheny.

"a good drubbing": Letter to Roseboro', July 19, 1932, Allegheny.

"subconscious": IMT, talk at Pen and Brush Club, May 24, 1934, ms., Allegheny.

226 "his struggle," "He practically . . . me so": Letter, January 18, 1939, Allegheny.

"always searching . . . truth": note from Phillips, Smith.

"too pious . . . cocksure": Letter from Roseboro' to McCormick, November 18, 1938, Allegheny.

226–27 "I looked with hope . . . on her side": Letter from Baker to McCormick, March 14, 1944, Allegheny.

CHAPTER 20. THE FINAL CHAPTER

228 She hoped to make it to ninety: Letter to Carrie Chapman Catt, November 18, 1937, Allegheny.

"Mr. Parkinson": note, Smith.

"great personality": clippings folder, IMT at 80, Allegheny.

"listened as if we'd . . . before": Brady, 252.

230 "wild and wavy lines": Brady's phrase, 253.

"seems to me to . . . importance": Brady, 252–53.

"Mr. Parkinson . . . normal": note, Smith.

232 "I am glad you said . . . preparing": Letter to Phillips, Smith.

"I thought I had things . . . apple cart," "only for a call . . . fall": Lyon, 410.

233 "cool, well-trained . . . masculine," "handsome . . . humanity": *Villager,* February 17, 1944.

"The American people . . . forgotten": Lyon, 411.

234 "limitation of mind": Jane Addams, quoted in Brady, 203.

Bibliography

SELECTED WORKS BY IDA M. TARBELL

PDFs of many of Tarbell's works can be found at www.unz.org/Author/TarbellIdaM.

SELECTED BOOKS, LISTED CHRONOLOGICALLY:

A Short Life of Napoleon Bonaparte. New York: S. S. McClure, 1895.

Madame Roland. New York: Scribner's, 1896.

The Life of Abraham Lincoln. 2 vols. New York: McClure Phillips, 1900.

The History of the Standard Oil Company. 2 vols. New York: Macmillan, 1904.

He Knew Lincoln. New York: Doubleday Page, 1907.

The Tariff in Our Times. New York: Macmillan, 1911.

The Business of Being a Woman. New York: Macmillan, 1912.

The Ways of Woman. New York: Macmillan, 1915.

New Ideals in Business: An Account of Their Practice and Their Effects upon Men and Profits. New York: Macmillan, 1916.

Life of Elbert H. Gary. New York: Appleton, 1925.

Owen D. Young. New York. Macmillan, 1932.

The Nationalizing of Business 1878–1898. A History of American Life, vol. 9, edited by A. M. Schlesinger and D. M. Fox. New York: Macmillan, 1936.

All in the Day's Work. New York: Macmillan, 1939.

SELECTED ARTICLES, LISTED CHRONOLOGICALLY:

"The Arts and Industries of Cincinnati." *Chautauquan,* December 1886, 160–62.

"Women as Inventors." *Chautauquan,* March 1887, 355–57.

"Women in Journalism." *Chautauquan,* April 1887, 393–95.

"Pasteur at Home." *McClure's Magazine,* September 1893, 327–40.

"In the Streets of Paris." *New England Magazine,* November 1893, 259–64.

"The Identification of Criminals." *McClure's Magazine,* March 1894, 355–69.

"Napoleon Bonaparte." *McClure's Magazine,* November 1894–April 1895.

"Abraham Lincoln." *McClure's Magazine,* November 1895–November 1896.

"The History of the Standard Oil Company." *McClure's Magazine,* November 1902–July 1903; December 1903–October 1904.

"John D. Rockefeller: A Character Study." Pts. 1 and 2. *McClure's Magazine,* July 1905, 227–49; August 1905, 386–97.

"Commercial Machiavellianism." *McClure's Magazine,* March 1906, 453–63.

"Tariff in Our Times." *American Magazine,* December 1906, January 1907, March–June 1907.

"Roosevelt vs. Rockefeller." *American Magazine,* December 1907–February 1908.

"The American Woman." *American Magazine,* November 1909–May 1910.

"The Uneasy Woman." *American Magazine,* January 1912, 259–62.

"The Business of Being a Woman." *American Magazine,* March 1912, 563–68.

"Flying — A Dream Come True!" *American Magazine,* November 1913, 65–66.

"The Golden Rule in Business." *American Magazine,* October 1914–September 1915.

"Florida — and Then What?" *McCall's Magazine,* May–August 1926.

"The Greatest Story in the World Today." *McCall's Magazine,* November 1926–February 1927.

"As Ida Tarbell Looks at Prohibition." *Delineator,* October 1930, 17.

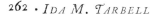

Sources

Allen, Frederick Lewis. *Only Yesterday.* New York: Harper & Row, 1931.

Baker, Ray Stannard. *American Chronicle.* New York: Charles Scribner's Sons, 1945.

Bausum, Ann. *Muckrakers.* Washington, D.C.: National Geographic, 2007.

Beatty, Jack. *Age of Betrayal.* New York: Alfred A. Knopf, 2007.

Bender, Thomas. *New York Intellect.* New York: Alfred A. Knopf, 1987.

Boyden, Albert. *Reminiscences and Tributes.* New York: privately printed, 1926.

Brady, Kathleen. *Ida Tarbell.* Pittsburgh: University of Pittsburgh Press, 1989.

Calkins, Earnest Elmo. *They Broke the Prairie.* New York: Charles Scribner's Sons, 1938.

Camhi, Jane Jerome. *Women Against Women.* Brooklyn, N.Y.: Carlson, 1994.

Chernow, Ron. *Titan: The Life of John D. Rockefeller, Sr.* New York: Random House, 1998.

Colburn, David R., and George E. Pozzetta, eds. *Reform and Reformers in the Progressive Era.* Westport, Conn.: Greenwood, 1983.

Cotkin, George. *Reluctant Modernism.* New York: Twayne, 1992.

DeNevi, Donald P., and Helen M. Friend. *Muckrakers and Robber Barons.* Danville, Calif.: Replica Books, 1973.

Dolson, Hildegarde. *The Great Oildorado: The Gaudy and Turbulent Years of the First Oil Rush; Pennsylvania, 1859–1880.* New York: Random House, 1959.

Douglas, Ann. *The Feminization of American Culture.* New York: Farrar, Straus and Giroux, 1977.

Filler, Louis. *Crusaders for American Liberalism.* New York: Crowell/Collier, 1961.

Franke, Warren Theodore. "Investigative Exposure in the Nineteenth Century." PhD diss., University of Minnesota, June 1974.

Giddens, Paul H. *The History of the Oil Industry.* New York: Macmillan, 1938.

———. "Ida Tarbell, Her Research Assistant . . ." *Oil Field Journal*. Reprint. Titusville, Pa: Drake Well Museum, 2002–2003, 39–47.

Graham, Jane Kirkland. *The Duchess of New Dorp*. Danville, Ill.: privately printed, 1955.

Hamilton, Virginia V. "The Gentlewoman and the Robber Baron." *American Heritage* 21 (April 1970): 78–86.

Helmreich, Jonathan E. "Ida at Allegheny." *Oil Field Journal*. Reprint. Titusville, Pa.: Drake Well Museum, 2002–2003, 6–19.

Henry, J. T. *Early and Later History of Petroleum*. New York: Augustus M. Kelley, 1970. First published 1873.

Hofstader, Richard. *Age of Reform*. New York: Vintage, 1955.

Johnson, Gerald W. *Incredible Tale*. New York: Harper, 1950.

Kochersberger, Robert, Jr. "French Lessons." *Oil Field Journal*. Reprint. Titusville, Pa.: Drake Well Museum, 2002–2003, 20–27.

Lears, Jackson. *No Place of Grace*. New York: Pantheon, 1981.

———. *Rebirth of a Nation*. New York: Harper, 2009.

Lewis, Alfred Alan. *Ladies and Not-So-Gentle Women*. New York: Diane Publishing, 2000.

Lloyd, Henry Demarest. *Wealth Against Commonwealth*. Englewood Cliffs, N.J.: Prentice-Hall, 1963. First published 1894.

Lutz, Tom. *American Nervousness*. Ithaca, N.Y.: Cornell University Press, 1991.

Lyon, Peter. *Success Story: The Life and Times of S. S. McClure*. New York: Charles Scribner's Sons, 1963.

McClure, S. S. *My Autobiography*. New York: Stokes, 1914.

McLaurin, John J. *Sketches in Crude-Oil*. Franklin, Pa.: privately printed, 1902, www.archive.org/stream/sketchesincrudeo00mclarich /sketchesincrudeo00mclarich_djvu.txt.

Mott, Luther. *A History of American Magazines*. Cambridge, Mass.: Belknap Press of Harvard University Press, 1968.

Nasaw, David. *Andrew Carnegie*. New York: Penguin, 2006.

Nevins, Allen. *Study in Power: John D. Rockefeller*. New York: Charles Scribner's Sons, 1953.

Nevins, Allen, and Frank Ernest Hill. "Henry Ford and His Peace Ship." *American Heritage* 9, no. 2 (February 1958). www.americanheritage .com/content/henry-ford-and-his-peace-ship.

Pelletier Library of Allegheny College. "Ida Tarbell" (home page), tarbell .allegheny.edu/index.html.

Pomper, Gerald. *Ordinary Heroes and American Democracy*. New Haven, Conn.: Yale University Press, 2004.

Rice, Judith A. "Ida M. Tarbell: A Progressive Look at Lincoln." *Journal of the Abraham Lincoln Association* 19, no. 1 (Winter 1998), www .historycooperative.org/journals/jala/19.1/rice.html.

Rockefeller, John D. *Random Reminiscences*. Garden City, N.Y.: Doubleday, 1916.

Roosevelt, Theodore. *Theodore Roosevelt: An Autobiography*. New York: Macmillan, 1919.

Sedgwick, Ellery. *The Happy Profession*. Boston: Little, Brown, 1946.

Skaggs, Merrill M. "Viola Roseboro': A Prototype for Cather's *My Mortal Enemy* (Critical Essay)." *Mississippi Quarterly* 54, no. 1 (Winter 2000/2001): 5.

Steffens, Lincoln. *Autobiography of Lincoln Steffens*. New York: Harcourt Brace, 1931.

Stiles, T. J. *The First Tycoon: The Epic Life of Cornelius Vanderbilt*. New York: Vintage, 2010.

Tomkins, Mary E. *Ida M. Tarbell*. New York: Twayne, 1974.

Trachtenberg, Alan. *The Incorporation of America: Culture and Society in the Gilded Age*. New York: Hill & Wang, 2007.

Treckel, Paula. "Ida Tarbell and 'The Business of Being a Woman,'" tarbell .Allegheny.edu/treckel.html.

Veblen, Thorstein. *The Theory of the Leisure Class*. Mineola, N.Y.: Dover, 1994.

Weinberg, Arthur, and Lila Weinberg, eds. *The Muckrakers*. Urbana: University of Illinois Press, 1961.

Weinberg, Steve. *Taking On the Trust*. New York: W. W. Norton, 2008.

White, William Allen. *The Autobiography of William Allen White.* New York: Macmillan, 1946.

Wilentz, Sean. *The Rise of American Democracy.* New York: W. W. Norton, 2005.

Wilson, Harold S. *McClure's Magazine and the Muckrakers.* Princeton, N.J.: Princeton University Press, 1970.

Yergin, Daniel. *The Prize.* New York: Simon & Schuster, 1991.

Ziff, Larzer. *The American 1890s: Life and Times of a Lost Generation.* New York: Viking, 1966.

Zinn, Howard. *A People's History of the United States.* New York: HarperCollins, 1999.

Photo Credits

Allegheny College Archives, Wayne and Sally Merrick Historic Archive Center, Pelletier Library, Allegheny College, Meadville, Pennsylvania: 42, 43, 45

Author's collection: 60

Chautauqua Institution Archive: 55

Fales Library, New York University: 128

Frederick Winslow Taylor Collection, Samuel C. Williams Library, Stevens Institute of Technology, Hoboken, New Jersey: 191

Ida M. Tarbell Collection, Pelletier Library, Allegheny College: ii, 4, 12, 17, 19, 23, 24, 47, 48, 52, 54, 63, 67, 75, 85, 109, 110, 139, 146, 158, 172, 175, 178, 179, 229, 231

Library of Congress: 31, 65, 71, 90, 98, 99, 100, 103, 105, 107, 127, 165, 169, 176, 182, 188, 189, 195, 197, 200, 201, 203, 207, 224

The Lilly Library, Indiana University, Bloomington, Indiana: 92, 93, 111, 119, 153, 215

The Millicent Library, Fairhaven, Massachusetts: 135

Pennsylvania Historical and Museum Commission (PHMC), Drake Well Museum, Titusville, Pennsylvania: 6, 8, 10, 15, 38, 74, 141, 148, 150

The Rockefeller Archive Center: 34

Smith College Archives, Smith College: 70, 91 (J. L. Lovell), 160 (Katherine McClellen)

Special Collections and Archives, Knox College Library, Galesburg, Illinois: 76

Ted Heineman: 51

University of Arizona Libraries, Special Collections: 221

Index

Page numbers in *italics* refer to photos or illustrations.

Emery, Lewis, 132
evolution, 26–27, 46

Finley, John Huston, 96, 111, 120
Flagler, Henry, 35, 143
Flood, Theodore, 53–55, *55*, 66–67,
     78–79, 114
French Revolution, 37, 63–64, 82, 92

Gary, Elbert H., 212–14
Great Depression, 219, 220

Harding, Warren, 209
Haskins, George, 46–47
Hazen, Charles Downer, *70,* 70–71,
     114, 115, 159, 160–62
Henderson, Jo, 66, 69, 73
Henry, Mary, 66, 69, 73
Hess, Ida, 20
History of the Standard Oil
     Company. See Standard Oil
     exposé
Hoar, George Frisbie, 104
Hoover, Herbert, 218, 219
Hubbard, Elbert, 151
Hubbard, Gardiner, 89–91, *90,* 92

industrialization. *See* big business

Jaccaci, August, 79, 216
James, Henry, *160,* 160–62
James, William, 64–65, 105
journalism. *See also* writing career
    men's acceptance of women
      colleagues, 62, 106

muckraking, 142
potential for political influence,
     61–62, 104, 106
requirements for women in,
     61–62, 81
Roosevelt's attack on investigative
     journalists, 167–68

Keller, Helen, 185

labor issues. *See* workplace
    conditions
Lincoln series and books, 94–99,
     100, 214
Livermore, Mary, 55
Lloyd, Henry Demarest, 121, 130,
     134, 145

Manifest Destiny, 29
Marbury, Elizabeth, 173–74
McCall's Magazine, 215–18
McClure, Sam S.
    admiration for Ida, 76, 94, 115,
      134, 150, 156
    affairs and indiscretions, *119,* 145,
      154–56
    approach to Ida to work for
      McClure's, 74–77, 84–86
    business expansion schemes, 76,
      87–88, 100, 111, 113, 156,
      163–64
    debt to Ida, 170
    demands and energizing effect
      on staff, 89, 100, 109–10,
      156, 165, 178

railroads (*cont.*)

  price fixing and kickback
     conspiracy, 35–39, 133–34,
     143, 177

  robber barons, 36

reform movement

  as focus of *American Magazine,*
     169, 179

  McClure's series on government
     corruption, 118

  potential power of women
     journalists, 61–62

  presidential candidate platforms,
     117

  Progressive Era, 117, 175, 191

  revolution as mechanism of
     reform, 37, 63, 83, 166–67,
     180

  during Roosevelt administration,
     118, 169, 197

religion. *See* Christian doctrine

Roaring Twenties, *207,* 207–8

Rockefeller, John Davison. *See also*
     Standard Oil

  autobiography, 146–47, 177

  death, 223

  evasiveness and secrecy, 120, 130,
     140, 159

  father of, 33, 131, 144, 149

  Ida's character sketch of, 147–49,
     148

  personal discipline, 33, 130

  philanthropy, 130, 144–45, 147,
     152, 223

  photos and artists' sketches of, *34,*
     146, 148, 150, 195

  religious conviction and practice,
     33–35, 131, 146

  risk-taking, 33, 35, 38

  self-confidence and ruthlessness,
     34

  silence concerning Standard Oil
     exposé, 147, *150,* 151

  start in oil business, 34–35

  wealth, 117, 129, 147, 195

Rogers, Henry H., 37, 39, *135,*
     135–37

Roland, Madame, 64, 66, 82–84,
     93

Roosevelt, Franklin Delano (FDR),
     220, 230

Roosevelt, Theodore

  assumption of presidency, 118

  fitness and activity, 103

  interest in Ida's Standard Oil
     exposé, 143

  investigation of Standard Oil, 117,
     157

  on investigative journalists,
     167–69

  photos of, *103, 169*

  as proponent of war, 102–3, 104,
     106

  reelection campaign, 196–97

  as reformer, 117, 118, 169

  on trusts and big business, 117,
     118, 169, *176,* 176–77

Roseboro', Viola